RICHCO

Sex.   Money.   Power.

I, Peter Rich dedicate this book to my son Little Peter.

"This is not an autobiography. Only I know what is true and what isn't."

Peter:

Memories can hold a person together, or they can rip you apart.

When I was a young man and still in the Navy I used to teach the new sailors how to resist giving in under the strains of torture. It was a cold war for sure, and it was my job to teach the guys to keep their heads and not crack. It's not as complicated as you might think. Just don't give in. Never give up.

You can learn to go somewhere in your head. Pain is only as powerful as you make it.

What many people fail to realize is they have the ability to control their own physical responses. If someone is trying to harm or torture you and you can keep your head, then they can't crack you.

The same goes for memories. They weasel their way into your day, popping up to harass you about the past, events you wish you could have prevented, opportunities that went by the wayside. There were good times and evil.

I tend more and more often lately to go off somewhere in my head as I attempt to put an order to the things that have happened over all the years of my life.

This is an account of the memories that make up the bulk of my life. Most of this account is true. Some of it is not. I don't want a memoir. I want to tell a story about the things I did and the things that I wish I did.

I am going to tell you how I have lived, how I have loved, how I have killed, and how I made my fortune. Any references to people alive or dead is purely a coincidence.

Maybe.

If you were to walk by me in the street you would think I was an ordinary man, dressed in ordinary clothes, and that's exactly what I want you to think.

My anonymity keeps me safe. I've made some dangerous decisions in my long life. Only a few people in the world know who I really am and what I have done.

Until now.

"To this day, I like to count the money. It turns me on."

1995

Elaine:

"Elaine, would you please come in here for a moment?"

His voice is deep and peaceful. He always sounds as if he hasn't a care in the world-- nothing at all like a man who ruled one of the single largest fortunes in the world. A man with secrets and a dangerous past.

Gentle, I think; his voice is gentle, like his touch.

I slide my black high heels back onto my feet and stand, straightening my gray dress.

The CEO's have been here one by one this week to talk about the progress of the various subsidiaries of RICHCO.

Brewster, the CEO of PB Holdings, had flown out this morning.

It's been a long week, but I try not to let it show. If the boss is working, then I'm working.

Peter is an interesting man. Normal enough, if normal is six feet tall and no fat. He's a man's man, who loves to fuck and to make money, and in that order. He often jokes about how the cash register is always ringing even while we have sex.

"Life's a bitch," he tells me, "but somebody's gotta do it!" Then he laughs with abandon and jokes sarcastically, "Here I am having sex and the till is still ringing!"

Actually, we were done having sex, and lying in bed chatting about some new acquisitions. It wouldn't have been too hot if he bragged like that during sex and the sex itself is amazingly hot. Though his sense of humor can be rather corny, but maybe that's one of his charms. He can always make me laugh.

Okay, so I understand it's a cliché, sleeping with the boss, but I don't care. And if I don't care then nobody else gets a say either. We are friends, we work together and we fuck. We have it worked out just fine, so there's no need to involve anyone else.

Upon entering his office, I receive an appreciative smile. Making sure to close the office door behind me, I return it.

He's sitting at his desk, the large windows behind him filled with the dim light of the setting sun. His tie is loose and his shirt sleeves are rolled up. The cufflinks he bought on our last trip to London are discarded on the edge of the desk next to the placard which reads, 'P. Rich'.

I think the universe played a great joke the day this bouncing boy was born with the surname Rich.

He's been counting again. Balancing the books.

His wife used to do this task, when she was alive. Peter always reminisces that she was the best book keeper.

"It always came out to the penny," he would say. "That's how meticulous she was!"

But now that she's gone he does the counting himself. It might seem strange, someone as rich and with so many companies managing this task on his own. Peter didn't mind being strange; plus I know the real reason he does it is because he likes to keep the bulk of his wealth a complete secret.

As far as I could tell, most of it was hidden away in offshore accounts, or was invested in various international businesses. Layers upon layers of investments and transactions, constantly moving to avoid taxation, but all legal and legitimate.

"I keep my nose clean," he would say.

I'm pretty sure that's why our headquarters are here in Dublin, for easier access to the world market, as well as the corporate tax incentives.

In Ireland, profit from income, capital gains tax and the corporation profits tax are all combined into one tax, which is neatly referred to as the 'Corporation Tax'. The tax here is also about a third of the rate in the United States. A tidy system, bringing lots of massive corporate companies to Ireland. In layman's terms, it's a heck of a lot cheaper to run your company over here.

The truth is I probably know more about Pete's assets than anyone else. He trusts me with a lot of information, but even I don't know everything. And I'm ok with that. I have enough to be getting on with just keeping track of the four main subsidiaries of RICHCO.

It's a private company split into parts and run by a few extremely qualified professionals. The four parts are real estate, oil, stocks, and transportation.

First and foremost is Peter's real estate empire, now known as RE, Ltd. Basically, this faction of the company is the oldest, though it has evolved many times over the decades. The CEO Peter put in charge of this gem is named Harold Clay. Harold is a 1969 graduate of West Point. He was quickly shipped off to Vietnam as a second lieutenant. During the war, Harold was wounded twice but finally got out of the Army as a Major. Pete discovered Harold after he came home to Harlem in 1975. Harold was doing pretty well for himself working in real estate in the New York area. Peter already owned some high-rise buildings and wanted to expand into all the major cities.

He tells me that Harold Clay was a tough son of a bitch and that's what he needed in order to handle Pete's real estate holdings and acquisitions throughout the world.

Next is PB Holdings, Ltd. This company focuses on fuel and is run by a man named Brewster Newy. Peter never had time to go to college, but he says he wished he could have gone to Harvard. Instead he hired a graduate of Harvard. Brewster holds a PhD in business, and for a time taught at his Ivy League alma mater. Peter saw his business talent and convinced him to help expand his oil and gas holdings dramatically. Brewster's expertise is in acquiring companies, though he has focused his efforts on those relating to oil and gas. He speaks Russian, like Pete, but also French and Arabic. He is like a rock star in the business world. Anyone who knows anything about foreign oil trading knows his name.

Karen Jones runs Money Trust, Ltd. I really look up to her, she can truly command a room. Especially a board room full of Wall Street suits. She is brilliant and graduated from the Wharton School of Business in 1971. After obtaining her MBA she went right to Wall Street. Pete tested her skills with a couple of successful transactions and then put her in charge of all his stock investments.

The fourth company, Get There Inc., is run by Edward Wong. Eddie was born in America of Chinese immigrants. He speaks Mandarin and many other languages, he like the rest of our team, is pretty much a genius. Pete only hires the best.

Eddie started working for Pete about fifteen years ago, which makes Eddie old enough to be my dad at least. Over the years he has built an empire throughout the United States, Europe, and Asia. This subsidiary of Pete's probably owns more vehicles than all other companies combined.

Peter brings me back to the present with a compliment, "You look beautiful today." Those green eyes of his twinkle at me from across the room.

"You say that every day." I sigh, but with a smile. It is nice to be appreciated.

"Well, it's true every day." He's not the least bit worried about sexual harassment in the workplace. My commitment to the company, is matched by my respect for the man, not that I would ever tell him that. But I think he can tell.

"When one works for RICHCO, it's for life," is what Pete always tells me. And why not, I'll admit it is a great life.

That doesn't mean bad things never happen. Bad things always happen, even to wealthy, powerful people. But Pete says he makes his own sort of justice if it's necessary.

It's true too, not just some boastful jest. Peter not only has influence in the government, but he has friends on the other side of the spectrum as well, dangerous friends. He says he always takes care of his people. He also says, "In this world, if you have money, you have power."

Well he should know, he's got more money than anyone else I know of.

I decide to sit casually on the leather couch by the book shelves. Feeling cheerful, I can't help but smile, remembering what we had done on the very same couch this morning, before anyone else had arrived.

"What's so funny?" He stands up and stretches his long legs. He's tall, and his hair is lightening-- not greying, just getting lighter. He's not strikingly handsome, but he is good looking; he's rough, like he's been in a couple of good fights. I think his eyes are my favorite thing. Well, the eyes and his smile. You can't have one without the other. When he smiles there's always a mischievous gleam in those green eyes.

Like now, as he stares intently, moving toward me. He looks good in a suit, but he also looks great in jeans and his leather jacket.

Pete still loves to ride on his Harley. As a matter of fact, the first time I met him that's what he was riding.

In 1986 when Harley Davidson Motorcycle company went public Pete bought up a bunch of stock. But that's not where his love the Harley came from.

He told me a motorcycle was the way he traveled as a youth. And he'd been fixing and working on these bikes since he was a kid. Back in his hometown forty something years ago, his first job was in a motorcycle shop fixing Harley's. A family friend gave him the job because he was so mechanically inclined. Honestly, it's as if this man can do everything.

Forty years ago! It doesn't seem possible. He seems ageless to me sometimes, but I know he was born in 1939, and that he served on a submarine during the Cold War. At best people usually peg him for forty-something. He certainly didn't move like he was in his fifties. He keeps very active, both at the gym and in the bedroom.

"Nothing, just, well..." I run my hand across the leather of the sofa and peer up at him. "Memories."

He doesn't join me on the sofa, but pulls me up to him, tangling his strong fingers in my hair as he positions my head, just rough enough to excite me but gentle enough to send shivers down my spine. We kiss long and slow. I can't help but reach up and wrap my arms around his neck.

We aren't usually this hands-on at the office. But as I said, it's been one hell of a week, and everyone else has gone home already. It's just us in the office now. Why shouldn't we blow off some steam?

God, the kissing! Who kisses this good? My job is awesome.

1995
Peter:

Somehow her presence always makes me reminisce.

It could be the smell of her rose perfume.

Or perhaps it's her youth. Twenty-five puts Elaine a full thirty-one years younger than me. When I was that age I had been married seven years already.

The times, they are a changin'.

Nowadays if a girl's engaged at twenty-five, people say she's too young to get hitched. Funny, my late wife was seventeen when we married and nobody said a thing!

I think it's her smile too. Elaine's constant cheerful smile reminds me of the young woman I married decades ago. Her smile and happiness, her young vibrant life. I pull back and trace Elaine's delicate lips with my thumb.

A kiss is your first introduction to a woman's body and you must prepare her for everything that awaits. Within that single physical moment, you must show tenderness, power, and the strength of your desire for her. Then she will be yours to have.

Simple.

When I was growing up there was a hay barn on the edge of town and a bunch of us kids from town would go out there to practice kissing.

I wonder if the owner ever knew?

I'm sure we left some impression in the hay.

There is nothing that keeps a young boy so preoccupied as a pile of hay and pigtails.

"Elaine." I use her name and physical presence to break away from my distractions.

Releasing her hair and trying to ignore the idea of what her hair would look like in pigtails I try get back to business. "I need a few hours, no disturbances." She smiles again and looks down at the leather sofa, misinterpreting my meaning.

With a minimal shake of my head she knows that's not what I meant. We get along well because we understand one another. She's intuitive, Elaine, and smart, too. She'll make a great CEO one day.

"Alright, I'll hold any calls." She leans over my desk to shut the ringer off.

"Why don't you leave for the day?" It's not a suggestion, and she nods.

I always make my tallies alone. As she leaves the office I dwell on the fact that while Elaine is my closest confidant, I am still the only person who knows it all. The vast holdings of my companies are well layered and secret.

Once a year, after meeting with all the CEOs of my companies I take some time to count my money.

A million dollars is a thousand thousands. A billion dollars is a thousand million and a trillion dollars is a thousand billion.

I made my first million by the time I was twenty-two. From there the growth was exponential. It took much less than twenty-two years to multiply that by one thousand.

As a kid I never had aspirations of being the richest man in the world. I wanted to be rich, of course, and that drive came early on from my grandfather.

You see, my father left when I was four years old. It wasn't like he ran off on us or anything. No, he served in the Navy during World War Two. And he came back after the war of course. But for a while there, he was stationed on a submarine in the Pacific.

That meant, growing up I spent a lot of time with my grandfather. He lived on the shore, and he taught me all kinds of things. We would hunt and fish on what was left of his land. His lessons were important to me and he had a joke or a saying for everything. One of my favorites was, "If you never quit you will always win!"

He believed very much in not giving up. There was this one time, when the town doctor decided to give up but Grandpa wouldn't let him.

In those days women usually had their babies at home, not in the hospital. A midwife or the town doctor would come to the mother's house to deliver a baby.

My father was their first born. When he was coming into the world the good ol' doctor shook his head in dismay. He said that my Grandmother was not going to survive the birth.

Well, of course Grandpa didn't like the sounds of that. His immediate response was to get the shotgun down off the wall.

It was simple he explained to the doctor, "If she dies, you die." And he stood there over the doctor with the shotgun and waited patiently for my father to be born.

Luckily my Grandmother pulled through, so the doctor didn't get shot. But that poor bastard had to keep going back to deliver babies, four in total.

As far as I know he only needed the persuasion once and the gun remained on the wall as a reminder.

My grandfather worked hard in his youth. He built a big successful company from the ground up. A commercial painting company. Gramps managed to gain contracts to paint most of the bridges in my home state. He was a blue-collar man who could do a good day's work. He also invested in and built spec houses.

You see, houses are built in two ways. Either a buyer purchases some land and hires a builder to put a house on that land for them. Or, a builder invests in land and builds a home banking on the fact that someone will eventually purchase the house when it's finished. This is a spec house, a home without an intended buyer.

Usually the houses are built in an affordable manner, since builders have much of the material and crew at their disposal. But they are not cheaply made and usually have features that make them appeal to a wide variety of people.

Today a modern spec house will often have multiple bathrooms and things like marble countertops. In my day it was Formica, but as I said, times change.

These are things people have come to expect in a nice home. Better than average. Adding these features makes the house marketable and therefore easier to sell.

My Grandfathers successful commercial painting company, along with the many homes he built and sold made him a millionaire by 1920.

He had a house on the shore with a couple of servants-- people still had servants then, it was perfectly normal.

It was 1929 when the stock market crashed that he lost almost everything. After the crash, banks started to fold. By 1931 Gramps had lost his unsold spec houses, since no one could purchase them. The banks took them over.

He kept working, of course. He never did give up. Plus, he still had his commercial painting company to run and profit from. After the Depression though, he never gained back the immense wealth from before.

I remember hearing that story for the first time. I remember it like it was yesterday.

We were walking to our favorite fishing spot, a little lake out in the woods. It was one of those fresh New England mornings when the dew clung to everything. The sun was just coming up, of course, since the early bird catches the worm. I had a bucket of worms in one hand and a fishing pole balanced on my shoulder. At seven years old, I stopped in my tracks to gaze up at the old man. Shaking my bucket and stating my big promise, "Don't you worry, Grandpa, I'll get it back."

I can hear his words as I sit and count my money.

"If you never quit, you will always win."

My final tally is one thousand and one billion dollars.

That's over a trillion dollars.

$1,001,000,000,000.00

I am richer than most countries. If only Gramps could see me now.

Oh, I got it back alright and then some.

"Have I ever told you about the first time I killed a man?"

Peter:

It wasn't really an option whether or not I would join the Navy. My dad had it all planned out and knew exactly when. The day I turned seventeen he brought me to sign up for the reserves.

I had trained my whole life for a career in the Navy. It's weird, but as a kid I never thought about how they were training me in the skills I needed to be a warrior.

Maybe it was the extensive training early on. Or maybe it was hard wired into me, but I was competitive from a young age.

This trait also made me calculating, because I liked to plan ahead, plan the win. I truly believe this drive to win and the ability to see it through to the end is the very backbone of any successful entrepreneur.

Diving, swimming, running and hard work made me swift and strong. Hunting with my grandfather from a young age made me stealthy and deadly.

I never miss a shot. It's actually a fun party trick.

One time when I was in my early twenties, I took my wife on a cruise, and they let us shoot trap off the back of the cruise ship. I never missed one, even with the boat moving up and down with the waves. Everyone wanted to know how I had done it, so I told them I was a hitman. And they believed me! The looks on their faces! It was priceless.

All joking aside, I wasn't a hitman, nor was I a sniper for the Army, though I could have been. I was in the Navy and I was a diver.

The training I received as a youngster set the stage for the deadly training I received in the Navy, and these skills saved my life many times.

I'm a lucky son of a bitch for sure, but killing a man is a lot easier if you've been acclimated from early on. There can be no hesitation when it comes to life and death.

The long and short of it is, my father trained me to be a weapon. He wanted me to go far in the military. And while I intended to join the Navy I also knew money was in my future. It was my goal to build a wealth generating company just like my Grandfather.

Dad wanted me to be a war hero. He had no idea what to do with money anyway. Jesus, my father was terrible with money!

My father was back from the war after two years. During war time, you went in and did your job until the war was done. Then you went home.

In early 1946 most of the guys who had kids and families were discharged. They got back as best they could to their previous jobs and families.

I was six, going on seven that year, and we moved into town, where my father opened a diving school. That was where I learned to dive.

Aside from being a champion runner, my father had been trained by the best in the Navy. I was an athlete too.

I don't remember a time when I couldn't outrun anyone, dive deep and swim far.

"Might as well've been a fish," my dad would mutter with a proud grin on his face.

Back then there was no such thing as the Navy Seals. At the time the special forces branch of the Navy was known as the UDT, or Underwater Demolition Team. That is just too damn annoying to say, so they called them Frogmen. They were the toughest sons of bitches you'd ever come across.

This is the distinction my father hoped for me when I joined the Navy.

The Frogmen were trained to destroy the metal barriers on the beaches that would prevent boats from landing. They could fight underwater and above. They were taught to think and react faster than other people. To become the best, they were pushed to their limits mentally and physically.

I'm not sure if most people even understand what this means, to push your body and stress your muscles every single day, so that not a day goes by without pain or fatigue. Unease becomes a part of who you are. You give up your body and comfort to the needs of your country, in order to become a combat machine capable of incredible things. Sometimes horrible things, but incredible nonetheless.

Nowadays people have some sense for what a Navy Seal is and what they are capable of, but very few men reach this distinction.

My father had a buddy from the war who was part of the UDT. He was a partner in my father's diving school and he helped train me. It did not escape me at the time how lucky I was. It was quite an honor to be trained by a war hero.

This Frogman taught me all sorts of things, neat things like underwater combat or not so glamorous stuff like how to get rid of cramps. Trust me, a cramp can kill you in the wrong situation.

Most importantly, he taught me how to keep my hands off his freaking wife! I'll never forget that! I was probably thirteen at the time, and his new wife was sitting by me. Even then I had an eye for pretty ladies.

She was a blond and probably around twenty years old. Let's just say I got a little handsy. That's when I found out exactly what a combat diver could do. He was over to us so fast, before I knew it he had my arm up and twisted so that I was standing suddenly with my back pressed against his front.

"Hands off, kiddo." He didn't raise his voice, but I heard him loud and clear!

Jesus!

The truth is, I wanted to be good at everything, not just scuba diving. Baseball, diving, kissing, running, making money, all of it. So when Dad said to swim harder, dive deeper, I did.

School was no different, but math was especially important to me. For example, when given a new form of math it became my mission to master it as quickly as possible.

My favorite teacher, the lovely Miss Ruth, saw in me some potential, so after a while she started tutoring me on the side. It was in this way I moved up into high school level math ahead of time. I liked school. It was easy for me, but it was also enjoyable. I would have gone to college, but the Navy was my path.

In my life, I have only focused on bettering myself. The successes I've had were because I never gave up and always worked at being better. It's not rocket science.

They say you can learn to do anything. Well, I believe that to be true. If you can't find someone to teach you, then get a book, and then work at it until you're good.

"Nothing's impossible if you know how to do it!" My grandfather had the best sayings. He was so corny. That one always made me laugh.

The point is, you can't just sit around waiting for things to happen to you, or complaining about what you can't do. Be resourceful! Work hard! Trust me, it's a handy way to build an empire.

1995
Elaine:

It's a rainy day in Dublin. What else is new, it rains here for approximately half the year. That's alright with me-- at least the winters aren't so bad. Back in New England where I grew up, the winters are terrible. Sometimes one winter storm will dump a foot or more of snow.

It's raining pretty hard, but I am met with an umbrella by Thomas. He is the doorman at the hotel where we live while in Ireland.

It's funny, Peter owns buildings all over the world, but unless we are home in the States or at his Caribbean bungalow we stay in hotels. He says Barb, his wife, liked to stay in hotels because they were always clean and there were people there to wait on you and make you feel like royalty. This hotel certainly accomplished that.

Thomas greets me with, "Hello, Miss Elaine. Lovely weather we're having today." He receives the desired chuckle from me.

"Good evening, Thomas. I trust you are enjoying this spectacular day!" Thomas helps me collect my packages, since I've stopped at the post office and the bookstore on the way home. He then escorts me away from the car as the young valet Eoin jogs over.

Eoin looks lovingly at the 1977 Rolls Royce Corniche convertible I've just pulled up in. Pete's got a thing for Rolls Royce and this model is nifty. He always goes on about the huge motor and the five thousand revolutions per minute.

All it means to me is that this old car can go 120 miles per hour and that's plenty fast. Pete likes to drive real fast, but I am not such a dare devil.

I do love this car, however. It's a creamy vanilla exterior with soft doe-colored leather seats. It doesn't look as impressive all closed up, but again with the rain.

As he hands me a ticket I tell him, "Enjoy! We just acquired that one."

His appreciation of the vehicle is apparent. "It's beautiful! And I'll have her all dried for you when I get under cover, Miss."

"And still with the Miss," I reprimand him jokingly. "Elaine, please." I hate it when people get too formal with me. I was raised in the country and deep down I will always be a farm girl.

"Yes, Miss." Eoin falters again then laughs, embarrassed, "I mean Elaine."

I shrug and smile at him, everyone has their habits.

As we reach the safety of the lobby Thomas shakes out his umbrella while he lectures me good-naturedly.

"That poor Eoin, I don't know what he loves more-- that fancy car or you!"

"Oh, hah, very funny." This is how Thomas and I get on, we joke with one another. "Obviously, he loves the car more!"

At the front desk I make sure there are no messages and order some dinner to be brought up, complete with a bottle of champagne. It's Friday night after all, at the end of a very successful quarter. Why not celebrate?

On the way up to my room I think about what tonight would look like if I were still back home, if Peter had never found me. My last evening class would just be starting; I would be in ripped jeans, not the latest Calvin Klein off the runway.

When I first met Peter, I was distinctly upset by him. All he did was talk about how pretty I was and make silly jokes about life, politics, and his sexual exploits. It didn't take me long to realize that this is how he presents himself. Not just to women as many people think, but to the whole world. He does fit the power hungry, sex hungry, meat and potatoes stereotype, but there's more to him than the merry jokester at the forefront. Underneath it all is a complicated workaholic with quite an amazing story to tell.

He really is a serious person once you get to know him.

He's also incredibly intelligent and startlingly mysterious. It's true! How many sixteen-year-old boys do you know, who have successfully started a company that thrives and lasts decades. A company that becomes the corner stone for a multi-billion-dollar empire? Not many I'm sure.

I've spent the better part of two years piecing together his past, and the results are nothing short of fascinating. Aside from his early success in real estate development, he also served in the Navy and has the highest government clearance possible. I think it's called "Q". Top secret sort of stuff.

I have no idea why it's called "Q" but I guess it's the type of clearance the Secret Service has, and people like the Inspector General. Well there you go, Pete has got his secrets, I often wonder if I'll ever know them all?

One time when I wouldn't stop bugging him about whether or not he was a spy, he made up this elaborate ruse where I had to "deliver" a special package to an "operative" on the "inside".

I ate it up, and agreed to help immediately.

It was exhilarating and terrifying. I remember standing in this swanky bar dressed to the nines sipping a martini, "shaken not stirred." I was playing spy all right! But I was incredibly nervous. What if something went wrong? What if I got caught? What if the world blew up because of me!

I was trembling slightly by the time the "informant" got there. He delivered the coded sentence that allowed me to know it was him: "The weather tonight is so disagreeable. If only we were in Morocco."

I was to respond, "But we are not in Morocco, darling," and then I was supposed to lean over, kiss him, and slip the top-secret package into his jacket.

Instead I jumped a foot in the air as he spoke, turned toward him, spilled my martini and mumbled, "Darling, it's not Morocco." Then I kissed him clumsily on the cheek and handed him the brown paper wrapped package outright. Anyone who cared to notice saw the ridiculous exchange. I failed espionage 101.

In the end, the package was full of Hershey's bars and Pete was in the corner of the bar laughing in a heap.

He thinks he's so funny. We sat in the bar that night with the actor/spy and ate chocolate bars for dessert.

Honestly, you'd think Pete had nothing better to do then play pranks on me. But he does much more than blow off steam.

He is a top-notch businessman and a humanitarian. We have many non-profits and scholarship programs.

Actually, working with RICHCO's charitable organizations is one of the best parts of my job.

I'm more than a secretary or assistant, I'm his right-hand man. Where he goes, I go. He is my mentor and my friend.

When I first agreed to work for him I vowed we would never sleep together. But I was wrong. I was wrong about a great many things. The world is not so easy to understand, but I am beginning to see things from his distinctly different point of view while he teaches me about the politics and power of money and of course the secretive world of candy bar espionage.

Two years ago, I was just about to turn twenty-three. I was a student in college and a waitress at a greasy spoon diner. On scholarship at the local university, I had just enough money in the bank to pretend it was "savings".

My plan was to get rich and go places! Show all the small town narrow-minded jerks I'd grown up with what real success looked like. But my plans were similarly small minded, at the time I didn't know what real success looked like.

Growing up my parents were hard-working blue collar folk. They taught me college was the way to success. They had never been to college. In their minds this step was what they had missed on the big ol' ladder to success and riches.

You can imagine, then, their disapproval when I dropped out a semester before graduation to accept a position at RICHCO, a company they had never even heard of, and probably never would.

The day I met Pete I was beyond tired. My schedule was full time everything. A full-time school, full time waitress, full time no sleeping schedule.

I ate the free food from the diner to save money. It was one meal per shift and as much coffee as I could drink. So, I ate one meal a day and subsisted the rest of the time on my large travel mug of cold coffee and cream.

Forgoing a car also saved me cash. I walked everywhere. Every weekday afternoon I'd walk, sometimes run, forty minutes to class, hauling a ton of text books and splashing my cherished coffee. I had it in my head that if I saved and sacrificed early on there would be a payoff.

This is what I told Pete when he asked me why I didn't buy a car with my savings or why I ate only at work. He liked to sit at the counter and talk to me about my plans, about money, and about real estate.

What really started our friendship, I think, is that Pete saw a little of himself in me. Now that I know more about his life, I understand that Peter believes in the same sacrifice.

But mostly he believes in hard work. At the age of sixteen he sacrificed what was left of his childhood in order to build his first company. Later he and his wife purposefully lived frugally, in order to have more capital for their early investments.

For instance, Pete once told me about how his wife saved over a month just to get a dollar for something special she wanted. It wasn't that she didn't have a dollar. No, they had money and they owned property, and Pete was getting a regular pay check from the Navy. However, all the money was allocated to certain investments and plans for their future, and of course paying the wages of Peter's building crew. Those things came first. Therefore, if Barb wanted something extra, she would save a nickel here or a dime there after all the other obligations were fulfilled.

Peter does not believe in credit. You buy what you can afford or you don't buy.

All I know is my overzealous work ethic appealed to Peter, and he got the idea to hire me.

So instead of working and saving and graduating, I jumped head first into the complicated world of RICHCO.

I'll never forget the first day he walked into my diner. He looked nothing like the owner of an international company. He had on jeans and black boots. His leather jacket looked worn but well cared for. On the back of the jacket was a kick-ass skull and crossbones. Those green eyes locked onto mine and we began our dance.

He would stop by sporadically, park his motorcycle outside and stay for breakfast, sometimes it was lunch. I hadn't known at the time he was splitting his time between multiple countries and time zones.

Eventually I started to take my breaks so we could eat together. He always had a joke to tell or a bit of wise guy advice. Hidden lessons, to be found under layers of sarcasm and sexual innuendos.

When Peter eventually asked me to work for him, I didn't hesitate to say, "Yes!" But I did add, "But don't expect me to sleep with you!"

As I turn the key and enter my hotel room I remember the comment with a sharp laugh. "He always gets what he wants!" I chirrup. I'm not upset, just flabbergasted as I often am when it comes to Pete.

"Excuse me, Miss?" Behind me stands a startled bellhop. He has brought up the champagne.

I look him up and down. He's young and cute, cuter still for his Irish accent. Forget about rain, Dublin was a fabulous place! If only I could be as flippant as Pete when it came to sex.

"Well," I think to myself, "flirting is harmless."

Why not? I fling the door open and let him enter, while taking off my long black trench coat.

Messing up overly neat hotel rooms gives me great pleasure, so the coat gets dumped haphazardly over an arm chair by the fire. My bra is back at the office somewhere. Both the bellboy and I are acutely aware of its absence, it being such a cold day.

"Let him look!" I think. How bold I'm becoming.

Indicating with a gesture where to set the bottle, I find some cash from my purse. He looks flushed as he takes the generous tip, his hand lingering against mine. Touch can be so electric. Our eyes meet momentarily. His sparkle with anticipation.

Wishing him a good night, I shut the door.

Not so bold after all.

Time for a shower. Peter would be back before long.

Needless to say, Pete has changed my world. Real wealth had been so far out of my comprehension before. I was focusing on the wrong aspects of wealth. Cars, houses, black AmEx cards. Just the stuff and the pay check I would need to get it.

But if you can make money even while you aren't actively at an office or physically working, that's when you can begin to acquire real wealth.

Peter often jokes that he has a hard time spending even a fraction of the money he makes. A hundred thousand dollars is nothing to him, a million much the same. I used to be so narrow-minded.

We became friends first. He would stay later and later at the diner, and at the end of my shift sometimes he would take me on his motorcycle to class, or sometimes we drove in a Rolls Royce or a Mercedes. You might be starting to guess that Mr. Pete has got a thing for cars.

I'm just beginning to wonder where Pete is when he finally shows up. He seems to be in a good mood, I guess he had a good time counting.

The dinner cart has just arrived as well, but we leave it to get cold.

He has this way of approaching a woman's body that still catches me by surprise-- the only way I can describe it is devotion. He's a worshiper of the female form. He's a big man, not just tall if you know what I mean, but I've never felt pain with him, only pleasure. He takes his time, and coaxes my body to relax until we fit together perfectly.

He says it's most important to be patient and pay attention. He pays close attention to my needs, and adjusts to even the subtlest response from my body.

The first time we had sex I was a little nervous. This was my boss and my friend-- and he was older, and huge! But he kissed me softly and used his hands, lips, and tongue to tease my body. He kissed me for the first time, introducing me to the skill of his tongue. Working his way down my body, my neck, my nipples, my stomach and inner thighs. His tongue can do amazing things.

In the past with other partners I'd sometimes have trouble staying focused. My mind would wander. I'd think about what else I needed to do for school, or about how I needed to do laundry before work the next morning. But with Pete I'm always present. There's no way not to be, while being the object of such reverent sincerity.

When he walks in I'm dressed only in lace as I pop the champagne and sip the overflow directly from the bottle. So classy.

"Mmm, you smell nice." He caresses and then kisses my neck, leaving a trail of goosebumps that mark a trail to all the sensitive, secret places of my body.

Pouring champagne had been my ultimate goal, but I am spun around for one of his skilled kisses. My panties are castoff with one sure movement. Down to the floor with them, another mess that I enjoy the story of.

What must the house keeper think of our rooms? Coming up for air, I can't help but laugh out loud without a care.

He always gets what he wants, but then again so do I.

"When God made little boys, he made them out of string, he had a little extra so he left a little thing. When God made little girls, he made them out of lace, he didn't have quite enough so he left a little space. Thank God!"

Pete:

As a little kid, I was always taking things apart. Nothing was safe in the house. It drove my mother furious! I took apart anything I could get my hands on-- bikes, radios, typewriters.

Funny story, I helped create the typewriter ball-- as a grown up, not as a child. Early typewriters had forty-nine letter keys attached on narrow metal arms. A typewriter ball is more economical and also the darn keys don't get tangled if you type to fast.

It's a ball with all the letters of the alphabet on it that rotates to make impact with the paper. Seems simple now that it's a thing, but that's how the world works. Everyone can see how simple it is after someone else thinks of it, and yet they always declare, "Why didn't I think of that?"

Taking things apart is important. It's good to see how things fit together, how they work. To this day, I like to break things down to simplicity and then rebuild them, hopefully better than before.

My father really loved cars, and by extension so did I. I still do, too. Elaine thinks it's funny, but I see how much she loves to drive the antiques. They are beautiful machines, and I do appreciate beautiful things.

Not long after Dad's return from the Navy he took up a hobby of stock car racing. In our spare time we would rebuild old Fords together, beef them up and ready them for racing on the track.

After a couple years I started to get smarter about what those engines were capable of. My dad and his buddies would always swap stories in the evenings over a beer and cigarettes.

Mr. Burt was a Harley Davidson dealer, so he knew about mechanics. Mr. Burt and his wife were good friends of my parents, and some nights after dinner while the wives were chatting in the kitchen sipping coffee, I would sit in the garage while my father and his friends went on about carburetors, combustion versus compression, and horsepower. I don't even know if they noticed me half the time, but I was there alright, listening closely and learning.

And of course, there were manuals. Tons of greasy old manuals just laying around the garage. When I could read well enough I got to obsessing over the sections in the auto books like other young boys obsessed over comic book characters.

And so, it turned out that as a kid, there were few things as important to me as racing.

Well, racing and baseball. I got pretty good at baseball, too. Since I hadn't yet experienced a woman (and not for lack of trying), I instead focused my time on sports and mechanics. School was easy for me so that didn't take up much of my time at all.

As a matter of fact, it was in Miss Ruth's eighth grade math class I came up with an idea to help my father build an engine that would win and keep winning. Just like Grandfather told me, "Second place is just another way to say first loser."

It was nearly the end of the school year so it was hot as hell in that stuffy classroom. I remember it vividly. Miss Ruth was going on and on about fractions, which I had already mastered, so I was spending this particular class daydreaming about building the most powerful engine for my car. Staring at the back of little Katerina's head and all her pretty brown curls, I started swinging one foot back and forth, back and forth.

"Hey, Pete, stop kicking my chair," little Katerina hissed at me, only turning her head a fraction, but nothing missed Miss Ruth's attention.

"Alright, class, let's focus." She addressed the room but I knew her comment was intended for us.

"Sorry," I whispered back to Kate. Her full name was Katerina, but everyone at school just called her Kate.

Her parents came here when she was twelve from a place called Ukraine. Kate didn't have a very strong accent, but I had a hard time understanding her father at times. By the time we were done with high school, Kate's accent had all but disappeared.

Everyone called them displaced people, or DPs. There was a whole bunch of people in those days running from war, trying to make a new start. We were friends, me and Kate, but she still didn't like it when I kicked her chair.

I put both my feet on the ground and picked up my pencil to finish my sketch. It was a cross section of two front cylinders that splayed out in a V pattern, just like the engine in our old green Ford. I added some shade to the piston and drew darker lines along the connecting rod and crankshaft.

My head leaning into my hand, I thought about how many more cylinders would have to be on submarine engines. How many times had I heard my father talk about the power those great big things were capable of?

The problem with our smaller engine was the lack of room for more power. Basically, a diesel engine works on compression in the pistons instead of the ignition of a spark like in gasoline engines. So, if the pistons were compressing more fuel the outcome would mean a greater amount of energy dispersed. And then it clicked.

On that hot June afternoon with the sweat dripping down my back, I had a eureka moment and started fidgeting in my seat again.

Kate sighed, and I whispered sorry again. She giggled into her hand and Miss Ruth glanced over, probably realizing focus would be hard to maintain on such a humid and sunny day. We should all have been outside, not cramped in the dusty classroom.

It was Friday and when that final period bell rang, we were off! Monday morning seemed ages away. I was thirteen years old with no plans for the weekend but baseball, swimming, and convincing my dad to use my plan for our new race car.

I walked with Kate on the way home. She listened as I told her about my idea for the car. She was really very polite and quiet. "It will be so fast, Kate! Wait until you see it. Just gotta figure out how to make it fit when we're all done."

"Duzhe dobre." She told me.

I remembered the word for good and knew she was complimenting me. "Spasybi!" I said enthusiastically thanking her. And Kate laughed at me happily.

She had slowly been teaching me how to speak her languages. Sometimes it was Russian, sometimes Polish. It was fun to think we had a secret language no one else at school understood. Also I'm sure she found it nice to converse in her native language.

She tested me again when we reached her house. "Harnoho vechora." She was wishing me a good evening.

"Spasybi vam tezh." You too, I answered.

"Bye, Pete." She laughed and I watched as her perfect curls bounced up and down with the rhythm of her steps. At her door she waved.

"Do pobachennya!" I yelled out and was gifted another smile. It was nice to make a lady smile.

When my family sat down to dinner that night, I completely ignored my little sister, totally looked past my mother when she asked how my day was, and honed in on the man at the head of the table.

"Dad! You know I am good at math." He looked up suspiciously, mashed potatoes halted in limbo between mouth and plate. I rushed on, excited. "Well, I have an idea for the Ford!"

"Okay, Pete, what's on your mind?" The fork finished its ascension.

"Okay," I started awkwardly. "So, I know everyone else is boring these one hundred horsepower flathead Ford V-eights to three and three eighths, but I figure we can go to four inches. If cubic inches are power, then more is better." I finished a little out of breath. It was a great idea! I hope he saw it, too. It was a pretty basic concept, but everyone had excuses due to the preexisting design of the engine we were working with. We didn't have the capacity to cast and build a whole new engine.

And so it was that Dad had his answer all set: "Look Pete, if you bore out any bigger you'd be into the water jackets." He shook his head a little and stabbed at his food.

Yes, the cooling system. We couldn't compromise that. We would need them for such a hot running engine. But I knew how to get around it.

"Of course I realize that, Dad! But you were a Navy mechanic, you know there are sleeves available that you can freeze press into the block. Then we could bore it out to four and *then* we would be able to use a much bigger piston. Nobody's at four inches! Our engine would beat any other. We'd win every time!"

The second mouthful of mashed potatoes fell back to the plate. And so it was. My father listened to me and he built that big engine.

"She was a goddamned Yankee, just like me!"

Pete:

I have known a lot of women in my time, if you know what I mean, but I've only loved one: my wife.

The woman that would become my wife acquired my love not by her body or the pleasure she could give me, although she did that very, very well. I fell for her because she was my equal. She was strong and smart and she gave me the greatest gift of all, my son.

But we haven't gotten that far yet. First, we've gotta talk about some of the girls that came before her. And I mean only some. If I had to outline my whole black book we'd be here for days!

Little Kate became my close friend in childhood, and her parents trusted me because of that early relationship, though they probably shouldn't have.

I used to take Kate out to dances and we had a good time 'practicing' together. It all started after the big race, on the day we tested out my engine.

Race day came sure enough. I had been talking about the alterations so much that Kate's dad brought her along so they could see how it all came together.

"It looks dangerous." Kate looked skeptically at the guts of the car totally exposed, the hood of the car having been the first thing to go. Nothing was bolted in right, but we had a lathe and a Bridgeport so the alterations were accomplished.

"Don't worry, little missy," said my dad, in his pre-race state of sheer excitement and adrenaline. "This car isn't any more dangerous than any of the others here."

Kate made a dubious face, glancing around at all the other souped up cars being tinkered on all around us. My father and Mr. Burt smiled at the joke, but I defended my car.

"This car is perfectly safe!" I felt an elbow hit my right shoulder and glanced over to see Burt smiling at me. They were just having fun.

I was all over full of nerves and just wanted the race to start. And that's when Kate pointed at the big 090 painted on the side of the car in white glossy paint.

"Oh Niner, like your nickname at school," she said with a smile. Katie didn't know why the guys on the swim team called me that; it was a sort of locker room joke. My dad had let me name the car since the engine was my idea. The engine was big too so the name seemed to fit. But I wasn't about to enlighten Katie right there in front of her father. Maybe later if I ever got her alone I could show her. My mind, of course, went there. I couldn't help it. Sensing the direction of my thoughts, Mr. Burt and my Dad thought it would be funny to pick on us.

"Yes, Pete, why don't you enlighten us as to how you got that nickname?" said Burt.

Kate's dad caught on and made a quick excuse about finding good seats. He steered his daughter away amid Burt and Dad's laughter. Kate looked back and waved, looking slightly bemused.

Thirteen is a strange age where you've basically got it all worked out from rumors, magazines, and older siblings. Puberty is in full swing and your body is changing real fast. When you're a boy-- I don't know about girls because I'm not one of them-- your curiosity takes hold of the better part of your brain and sex is all you can think about, with small breaks to race a car or finish some homework.

The guys on my sports teams, having this same dilemma, found it hard not to focus on a particular aspect of my physical appearance while in the showers. They decided my nickname should be 'Niner'.

We won all of the half mile dirt track races that year and I did love winning.

To add to the success, Mr. Burt decided I could have a shot working in his shop. I was young still but he knew I had a good head for engines. I accepted the job offer straight away.

Mr. Burt was a successful business owner like my grandfather. I knew he was a good man to know if I was going to amass a fortune.

As a matter of fact, Burt became one of my first investors and remained a mentor to me for years to come. And so, the 090 proved to be the catalyst which began my ascent to wealth, all from an idea I had one afternoon in math class.

"My father hit my mother once. I made sure he never did it again."

1995
Elaine:

When Pete started the American Patriots Fund, it was to take care of the families who had lost soldiers during the raid on Iran. It was established in 1981, and has evolved since then into a much bigger organization, which RICHCO still supports, among other charitable organizations.

But it's Peter's continued involvement in the local Women's Shelter from his home town that truly speaks to his sense of duty. His wife Barbara had the idea for the Women's Shelter, and together they built a safe place for abused women and their children to go when they had nowhere else to turn.

Both Peter and Barb had seen families torn apart by abuse and alcoholism. Pete told me a personal story once about how one night his dad got drunk and began hitting his mother. He said he was taller than his own father by then and gave him a real beating in return.

After that his dad never raised a hand to hit his mother again. Pete says they never talked about it either. His father just never hit her again.

But not all young sons have Pete's size, strength, or the courage to stand up to their abusers in this way. That's where the shelter comes in.

One of my duties as Peter's assistant is to organize and plan the annual fundraiser for the Women's Shelter. Pete has maintained the charity since the death of his family and now I have the privilege of helping to arrange the formal affair.

It's been fun. Almost like planning a wedding, except without the pesky getting married part. I've selected flower arrangements, and food. I've even got a new dress, black in defiance of all white dresses everywhere.

Brewster, the CEO of our oil and gas holding company, PB Holdings, was the one that came up with the idea of a high-profile guest. He was still in Ireland, and had popped in for a meeting with Pete before flying off to Russia.

As we've discussed; Peter likes to avoid media and limelight. So, he uses his CEOs as shields from any sort of publicity. Everyone in the corporate world knows the name of Brewster Newy, but hardly anyone knows the name Peter Rich.

Brewster Newy is a nice guy. He's a few years older than Pete and he, unlike my boss, looks his age. His hair's mostly grey and he's softer around the middle, but he wears nice suits so it doesn't show all that much. Brewster's married to a nice woman named Susan, who is a rather successful romance novelist. She spends most of her time at their home on Cape Cod.

When I first started with RICHCO we spent a week out there at the New England beach house. Brewster and Pete holed themselves up in the office speaking in Russian on a slew of conference calls, hashing out some big deal.

I hadn't learned much about business on that trip considering I can't speak Russian, but I did get a lot of kayaking in.

When Brewster took the reins of Pete's holdings company, he had taken an already wealthy Pete and moved him to the next echelon of super rich.

So, it surprised me when, on his way out of the office the other day, Brewster stopped by my desk and said, "Elaine, I'd like to come to your event."

I laced my fingers together and looked up at him. "The Women's Shelter event? In the States? Does Peter think that's wise?" I didn't want people seeing them up close. They had been colleagues and friends for decades, but not many people knew that. For some reason this move made me feel overly protective, though it didn't seem to bother the men.

"It will be alright, Elaine." Pete joined us. He smiled and slapped Brewster on the shoulder. "Why wouldn't I know a wealthy businessman? With all my world travels it wouldn't be too hard to believe. Besides, it will be good for press, and Mr. Money-Bags here can make a big contribution to our cause."

"Okay, boss, you got it." I shrugged. "Brewster, I'll send an invitation to your assistant."

"Great. I'll be at Harvard the day before; they've invited me to speak."

"Oh, fancy," I joke. "But you're going to be tired, Brewster! Russia, Boston, and then the dreadful drive to our party!" Though I know he is used to excessive traveling by now.

"It's not the drive I dislike," he responded, "it's the traffic."

"Christ," agreed Pete, "a drive that shouldn't take more than an hour takes four!"

"An hour." I scoff. "You drive too fast."

Brewster looks from me to Pete, questions in his eyes, but he knew better than to pry. The CEOs had been chosen for their expertise in their fields, but they had also been chosen for their discretion.

Peter extended his hand and they shook. Brewster said to us, "See you both next week. Travel safe."

"Same to you." I watched him walk out, then looked to Pete. "This seems different. You don't usually like to make a scene."

His eyes are playful. "I'm not gonna make a scene." He shoved a thumb in Brewster's direction. "Newy's gonna make the scene. It'll be great."

Oh well. I shrugged. Peter did make his own rules, and he could break them. Maybe he was getting tired of being so secretive. He had opened up to me after all.

"It was different then. People were different. We knew how to keep secrets."

1954
Pete:

Baseball was my favorite sport. I was also on the swimming team, but swimming was a part of my everyday life from childhood. It was just something I did, like breathing. Baseball on the other hand was totally mine. It was something I was good at because I had decided to practice and train. It helped that I had twenty-ten vision just like Ted Williams, a fact I was incredibly proud of.

Between my sports, the racing, and my new job at Mr. Burt's motorcycle repair shop, I had more than enough to keep me busy, but in early spring of my fourteenth year everything changed.

The high school football coach, Mr. Andy, was after me to play on his team. I had the proper physique for a football player, and at fourteen I was taller than most of my classmates and all muscle from my years of swimming and scuba diving. I knew though, football wasn't for me-- baseball was my sport.

I used to dream about being done with high school and playing major league baseball with the Boston Red Sox. I did get a chance to try out for a major-league team, the Colt 45's in the spring of 1960, but I turned down their offer to join one of their farm teams, because I was already married, had a kid, and a thriving business.

It was only a few years before that, before I was a business owner in my freshman year, that the football coach just wouldn't leave me be. He caught me heading toward the locker rooms one day just outside the gym.

"Pete," he says to me, "why don't you come out for football?"

"I don't know, Coach." I didn't want to seem rude. He was only looking after his team.

"Come on, Pete, you're tall for your age, I'd say over the summer you'll be close to six feet and I know you are very strong. You train hard with the swim team, I can tell."

"Coach, I don't particularly like football. You know baseball is my game. I only do well on the swim team because my dad and grandfather always pushed me. It's the scuba diving I really have to train hard for."

"You're not afraid, are you, Pete?" asked Mr. Andy.

I don't know why he thought a comment like that would bully me. Even then, I couldn't be bullied. "Coach, I am not afraid of anything or anybody," I replied, speaking slowly to drive my point. "I've never lost a fight and you know I can defeat any wrestler we have. I've had boxing lessons and my dad is a master diver who has forced me to train since he returned from the war. He taught me swimming for strength, diving for endurance and hand to hand combat both in and out of the water so that no one would ever push me around." It was a good verbal resume. I hoped it would get my point across.

He wasn't picking up on my hints. He actually said, "I still don't think you have the balls."

That was it. "Really!" I was a lot of things, but not a coward. Who did this guy think he was? If it was odd for a fourteen-year-old to react this way, I didn't know. Maybe this was the way he spoke to his team, but I wasn't his team and I never would be. Calling me a coward was the last straw. "Let's go out back. I'll show you a coward." I was dead serious and leaned forward. I was taller than him and looked down, straight into his eyes. That did the trick. His big man coach mask fell off his face and he took one step backwards.

I've never gone looking for a fight, but at a point like that there was no backing down.

"You know I would lose my job for that, Pete."

Not good enough for me "Okay, Coach, I'll tell you what. You pick your two toughest players and I'll take them both on at the same time."

Luckily, Mr. Jobba, another teacher was close enough to overhear the last part of our conversation and saved Coach his moment of embarrassment. Walking swiftly up the hall, the young teacher caught up to us. "Hey, Pete, got a second?"

"Sure, I've got time," I told Jobba. Coach turned and left without another word. I didn't see him much after that.

Jobba was twenty-two years old and a recent college graduate. He taught the business class to the juniors and seniors but I knew him as the baseball team's junior coach. He didn't really know shit about baseball but he had a seventeen-year-old girlfriend named Mary that I liked. She was hot.

He looked me up and down. "You should be a little calmer when addressing your teachers, Pete."

"He said I had no balls!"

Jobba laughed. "Well that was uncalled for." We started walking towards the locker rooms. "I've got tickets to the Red Sox game this Saturday. Think your parents would let you go? We could bring a couple guys from the team, too."

"Will Mary be there?" I asked, maybe seeming a little too eager. But Jobba just laughed and said she would be.

And so we drove up to Boston in Jobba's brand new 1954 Ford Sedan. The game was memorable. Ted Williams, "The Kid," was the star of the field. Of course! He was one of the greatest hitters who ever lived. He batted a .405 in 1941, and no one has done that ever since. The highlight of that day, however, if you can believe it, was not the baseball game.

After an day spent in the sun, shouting and throwing peanut shells, we were all pretty subdued. By the time we got well out of the city the sun was starting to set. Mary was sitting up in the front seat with Jobba. He had one hand on the steering wheel and the other arm stretched across her shoulders, totally at ease. It had been a hot sunny day. Mary had a bit of sunburn on the tip of her nose and across her cheeks, like she was blushing constantly. I liked it.

At some point, Mary asked to pull off for some beer. So Jobba stopped and got a quart bottle of Narragansett. Mary really liked beer, or at least the way it made her feel, and started drinking it right away, and fast.

We weren't back on the road long before Jobba decided to show her off.

"Mary, show the guys your tits." She laughed and kept at the beer, so pretty soon it did seem like a good idea to her. "It's hot anyway!" she declared, handing the beer back to us and facing the back seat, she unbuttoned her shirt.

I had been eyeing Mary all day, with her white button down undone a little more than was proper. The heat from the day built little beads of sweat on her chest. I spent most of the day imagining her naked. Suddenly there she was in reality, sitting in her bra, within arm's reach. So I said, "Mary, can I feel your titties?" Talk about balls! But Jobba didn't seem to care. In fact, he was encouraging us.

Mary seemed amused by how bold I was, and took the bottle of beer back. "I don't care, Pete." She climbed into the back seat, swapping with one of the guys. He immediately turned around to see what I would do next. Bold as anything, I helped her out of her bra. Her nipples were perfect: small, hard and pink.

Jobba seemed to be enjoying himself. "You can fuck her if you like, Pete." He started looking for a place to park. Mary smiled, so I guessed it was fine with her, too. When you are young, no isn't in your vocabulary. I helped Mary out of the rest of her clothes as well as my own. Mary grabbed my cock and said, "I've never seen one this big!" and the other guys laughed, saying, "Now you know why they call him Niner!"

I couldn't wait for the car to stop-- I fucked her while Jobba was still looking for a place to park. Then we all got out of the car. I felt compelled to play with her some more, this time slower. I wanted to watch how she reacted.

The other guys did her, too. I got the sense Jobba liked to watch. He never touched any of us guys, but he watched everything that happened.

Nobody even had a condom let alone thought about using one. The school or our parents never found out and none of us told anyone that I'm aware of.

Eventually Jobba got drafted by the Army and Mary got married real young. Sometimes I wonder what ever happened to her.

It had been a good day at the ball game, but I could have cared less about baseball after that. I never did move up to varsity that year because I was fucking Mary so often. She was my first.

"This one time I was beating the crap out of Randy—He had just gotten out of jail for breaking and entering. He thought he was tough, so he took a swing at me. Trust me he got what he deserved for that-- I might've killed him if Mr. Burt hadn't pulled me off him. Years later he worked for me as a painter, and a good one at that."

Pete:

Besides my grandfather's story to motivate me, there were two men from my hometown that helped me to begin my ascension into wealth.

Mr. Burt had already been impressed by my knowledge of mechanics, but shortly after hiring me in his shop he would become my first financial investor.

Then there was Mr. Bob. He was a businessman and entrepreneur who sat on the local bank's board of directors and also owned the town lumber company and coal facility.

He and his wife never had any children. I think that he eventually came to think of me like a son, and he taught me everything he knew about banking and being a business owner.

Mentorship is sadly becoming a thing of the past. I have tried multiple times over the years to find and foster a young entrepreneur. It has never worked out. Either my intentions were misinterpreted, or the person I vested my precious time in would become too big for their britches.

All of a sudden, I'm just an old man, and they don't need any more boring out dated lessons.

Elaine was and is different. She's smart but humble, and she knows that in business there is always something new to learn, as the market and products evolve. Elaine understands that hard work is always a part of being the boss. A good work ethic is not something I can teach to a person.

I could tell from the very start that she wasn't afraid of hard work. Most importantly, though, she tells it like it is. These are all qualities my first mentors saw in me. I hope my efforts with her are as effective as theirs were with me. I'm not getting any younger. I would have taught my son all these lessons if he had lived. He was a real neat kid, I would've liked to see what he'd have done with his life. Would he be like his mother, organized and meticulous, or more like me, with a good enough sense for business to run my company? Would he have been a ladies man? I'd like to think so, but these are things I'll never get to know.

What I do know is that Mr. Bob and Mr. Burt trusted me even though I was young, like I trust Elaine. She has those important qualities Bob and Burt could see in me all those years ago. Even as a kid I wasn't afraid of a long day's work. Most importantly, when it came to business I was straight forward and honest. I was sixteen when I decided to start my first business.

In 1955, the summer after my Sophomore year, my father and I built a new house. It was modest, just the right size for our small family, but it had some nice additions to it that a lot of houses at the time just didn't have, like hardwoods on the floors and for the cabinetry in the kitchen.

We built the cabinets by hand with the help of a local carpenter. There was no Home Depot back then, with any of those prefab particle board numbers. Everything had to be meticulously carved and made by hand. I don't think many in the younger generation have a sense for what this means. It took days of work to build those cabinets. In the end, they were level, and smooth, with all but the most minute imperfections. Those slight discrepancies the difference between manmade and machine. Making the finished product, not weak or wrong, but all the more beautiful, showcasing the individuality of the craftsmen who made them.

Everything in the house was like that, built with our hands. It was good hard work, that left me proud at the end of the day. Tired, so very tired, but exceptionally satisfied.

From the ground, we pulled large fieldstones as we dug the foundation. These rocks of all sizes were saved. Those very stones went into the large fireplace in the living room. I spent many winter mornings splitting wood for that fireplace. It was an essential part of our home, and many homes of the era. We used the fire to help get us through the long, hard New England winters.

Here's a lesson listen up. Work keeps you alive and well. As a boy, I wasn't given the luxury of sitting around saying, "I'm bored!" or "I'm cold!". If I was cold I would go outside and warm my body with the work of chopping wood, and then there would be the satisfaction of sitting by the crackling fire while snow piled up outside. If I was bored, I would find a way to stop being bored. Go off into the woods with my friends and hunt for game, or when I was older go off into town to hunt for women. Life is not boring if you are really living, moving, fucking. That is life to me and it is glorious.

As I said before, the house was modest. There were only two rooms at the top of the staircase. My room was to the right. Across the landing was my sister Lee's room. It was painted pale peach and covered with gauzy cream colored fabric. My room was austere in comparison. The plaster wall was painted the same off white as the rest of the house. I added no decoration. There was a twin bed and a simple desk. All the clothes I owned fit within the little closet I had framed out with solid oak molding, and stained a nice dark brown.

My mother out of desperation to add some decoration to the room had hung red flannel curtains on my one window. They went directly to the sill and were held back with matching ties. On the ground was a brown and cream colored hand braided oval rug. I think some aunt or cousin had made it as a wedding gift for my parents.

Downstairs was a bedroom for my parents. I don't think I ever set foot in that room after the houses completion, but I remember the song my mother was humming when she made the rather extravagant lace curtains, and matching pillows. She was very happy with the new house. We all were proud of the work we put in.

Of course, there was a large kitchen and there was one bathroom we all shared.

One afternoon while we were still building this house, little Kate popped by to see how the work was going. She wasn't so little anymore.

It was 1955. We were fifteen now and in high school. In our minds that practically made us adults. Now, when I would show up to take Kate out, my mind wasn't concerned with Polish lessons. I was focused on other things. Things that would take us on secluded hikes in the woods or sometimes we would sit by the pond speaking in our languages and I would undress Kate with my eyes. I don't know why her mother trusted me!

So, Kate stops by this one afternoon when I was in the kitchen working on the cabinets. Kate had on a pale pink summer cotton dress. Young women still wore full skirts back then. Now-a-days they only wear full skirts at their weddings, and sometimes not even then.

"Looking good!" She sounded impressed.

I turned and smiled. "Well thank you, I have been working out."

Kate shot me a wry smile. "I was talking about the kitchen, Pete!" She waved her hand at me as if to smack me if I were closer.

I laughed at her and wiped some sweat off my brow. It was a hot day and I didn't have my shirt on, but I found it and pulled it over my head. Kate had brought a Thermos filled with fresh lemonade. We went outside to find a place to sit and talk.

You know, it sounds like a scene out of a 1950s movie, and it might as well have been. It was the 1950's! And if you wanted lemonade you had to melt sugar into water and squeeze lemons. Or in my case, you needed to have a lot of girlfriends who would squeeze the lemons for you and show up in pretty fluffy dresses with their hair curled perfectly. We found a spot on the grass.

"Oh, Pete, I just wish my dad could build a house this nice for us to live in. I know it would make him so happy." She poured some of the cloudy liquid into the top of the thermos for me.

"Well, why doesn't he? It's not that hard." The lemonade was cool and just sweet enough the tart lemon flavor making me suck in my cheeks a little.

"Was it expensive?" She seemed excited at the idea of living in a house and not in an apartment in town.

"I think after the land, we are all in at about eight thousand dollars." I had been keeping track of the expenses, since I had a knack for numbers and my father couldn't be bothered with such things.

She whistled. "Too rich for me, Mr. Money-Bags."

I laughed; she was a funny girl. I tried to piece together a sentence. "Może dzień." I wanted her to be hopeful.

Kate looked at me strangely, trying to understand what I meant. Then she shook her head so that her curls bounced prettily and she corrected me like any good teacher. "Może kiedyś."

I thought about how Mary liked it when I pulled on her hair a little, and reached out to gently play with Kate's golden hair. She blushed and tucked her hair behind one ear. Then unexpectedly she leaned forward and repeated her correction in a whisper: *"Perhaps one day,"* she gently reprimanded me in Polish.

"Pete!" My dad stuck his head out the upstairs window. "Break time's over, Romeo!"

"Oh gosh!" Kate used one hand to cover her eyes embarrassed again. "See ya, Pete." She grabbed up her thermos and started to walk toward the road.

I couldn't let her get away that easy, so I chased after her and gave her a quick kiss on the check. "Wkrótce!" I tell her, which means *soon*. Well, that really got her blushing.

I whistled on my way back into the house. What a fun game this romance thing was. My dad was pulling his head back into the window, shaking it back and forth, but he had a smile on his face.

As I got back to work in the kitchen, it seemed to me that building houses wasn't too difficult. Just muscle and tradesmanship. In short, a lot of work. My father and I did everything in that house, including the electrical and plumbing.

But Kate was right, it wasn't just work. My father had the money for the supplies, and when we needed to hire an electrician to show us how to do something we had the means to do it. Money was the issue for so many families.

Kate's parents' problem bothered me. Just because a they were from another country and just starting out in a new place didn't mean they shouldn't have a home of their own.

And that's pretty much when I decided to get in the business of building houses. Only problem was no bank would fund me—money again.

I was too young the local bank said, too risky. But that didn't stop me, of course not.

There was a simple solution, and it could be addressed when I next went to work at the motorcycle shop. Mr. Burt didn't have a mortgage on his house or the building his shop was in. He also took back the financing on the motorcycles he sold. Meaning he would take the risk of financing his customer's new purchases on himself, not a bank.

This all meant one important thing: Mr. Burt had extra money available for investments. This is where I came up with my next brilliant idea.

At closing time, just a few days after drinking lemonade with Kate, I told him the plan. "You know, Mr. Burt, I've just finished helping my dad build our new house from top to bottom."

"Yes, Pete, it's a lovely house. You know I've always been impressed with your work ethic. Most kids your age are off getting into trouble."

I thought about all my time with Mary and wondered if he meant things like that, or if he was talking about drinking and drugs. Well, I didn't do those things, just Mary, and soon Kate.

Time to talk about business not think about sex. I shook my head. "I have a business idea."

"What's on your mind, Pete?" Mr. Burt flipped the Open sign to Closed and I handed him back the keys I had just used to lock the bay doors.

"I know a house can be built properly and still make a decent profit on it. It's how my Grandfather used to make money. He built spec houses. Well, I can work hard after school and on weekends and I know who to hire for the things I don't know how to do, or can't do well. Mr. Bob owns the best lumber yard around and he and I get along really well. All I need is the financial backing and the bank already turned me down, because I'm not old enough for a loan."

"You want me to finance your house building business?" Burt was smiling. I really hoped he was taking me seriously, because I didn't have time for jokes. I had a fortune to make. This was step one.

"Yes, sir," I said with confidence.

After that I went to Mr. Bob. As I said before he was the owner of the local lumber and coal company.

Because he also sat on the board of directors for the local bank, he already knew what I was after and that I had been turned down for a bank loan.

Mr. Bob was a power in town. Much later when I was twenty-one and out of the Navy he tried to get me on the banks board right alongside him, but at that point I wasn't interested.

We used to talk real estate because he had a broker's license. It was he who really inspired me to eventually begin my own brokerage. It really made sense after building houses for so many years that I should collect profits from all aspects of the real estate transaction. Also as a broker with other licensed agents working underneath me, I could collect money on all their sales transactions as well.

Mr. Bob had the nicest house in town, and that's saying something. There are a lot of beautiful mansions there. But he had no children and he had nothing to spend all his money on.

Not that I ever had to borrow money from him, just the lumber. I already had an investor before I approached him.

I said to him, "I'm going to build a house, Mr. Bob, and I need ninety days on my lumber. Mr. Burt is my backer and you know how strong he is financially."

With Mr. Burt's money in my pocket I had the capital to begin paying my crew, but if Mr. Bob could give me the lumber for construction on credit, then I would have a safety net. I wouldn't have to spend any money on supplies until there was a profit from selling the first house and I could pay a small crew to help with the work.

It all worked out pretty smoothly considering I was only sixteen. I'll never forget Mr. Bob's words: "I must be crazy, but I'm going to take a chance on you, kid."

I'll spoil the ending for you: his chance paid off. I started a successful business building single family homes. Because I was still in school and I couldn't do all the work on my own, I hired local tradesmen from town. They all liked me and thought it was real neat to work for a sixteen year old.

My only rules were no drinking on the job and be to work on time, and at the end of the week they got paid with a good check. I would meet them at the job site early and work a little before heading to school. Then I'd be back in the afternoon to finish out the day. I gave them Sundays off, but most of the time I still worked. I wanted the payout from the final sale.

It might not seem like a lot now, but we made $1,500 profit on that first house. In a time when someone making good money only made about $3,500 a year. Our profit was a large chunk of change.

Unheard of at the time, each house came included with a one-year unconditional guarantee. It was important to me because I wanted people to feel confident in the workmanship of the home even though they were buying it, in their eyes, from "just a kid".

I built and sold three houses the first year. Year two I tripled that number. My first business was officially a success.

"Some stuff you can't make up, honey. You just can't make it up!"

Pete:

I had this concrete guy named Jim. He was Mr. Jim and is not to be confused with my cousin Jimmy, who we will talk about in bit.

Mr. Jim owned and operated the local concrete company. He was reliable for the work and had a whole crew of guys working for him. His crew would pour the footings and foundations for my many houses.

Jim had a tendency to party hard and had a knack for getting into trouble over it. You see, this guy was married but he liked to sleep around. Who doesn't? But he was sleeping with the wife of one of his employees. One day this employee finds out about the affair and decides to get even. This is why I don't tell secrets-- I learned my lesson the hard way, but at least it didn't involve concrete!

Mr. Jim had a real nice red convertible, and next time I show up at a building site, there's Jim screaming, standing next to his car while the guy in a cement truck just keeps filling the car with wet cement. The car was ruined!

Honestly, I think Jim was lucky he wasn't sitting in the car when the cement went in. I don't think that would have stopped the other guy, he was so pissed off!

Barb probably never knew how often I slept around with other women. We never talked about it, and there was never any reason for her to question me. I don't kiss and tell.

I loved her, and we had a very healthy love life, but I never stopped seducing women. It didn't mean I wasn't in love with my wife. I've said it a million times: sex is sex. Love is different.

Then again, my wife was a very smart woman and she knew what kind of man I was when we first got together. 'A bad boy,' her friend Nancy had said, 'with a reputation.' The first time we made love, Barb had let me know she was aware of my conquests and even so she wanted me. We went on from there, never looking back.

She knew I was a dirty dog. She used to say it to me: "Pete, you have such a dirty mind!" She would ask me questions like, "How long do you think it would take you to seduce that woman?" She would point someone out across a restaurant, or on the beach. She'd say, "How long before you could get her into bed?"

I always answered honestly, of course, and say something to the tune of, "Maybe a day or two."

Well, anyway, my concrete guy Jim didn't have too many affairs after that one. His wife left him and he died not long after while on vacation in Florida. He drank himself to death.

"When I ride, I ride, and when I'm with you, I'm with you ... it means when I am with you, you have my undivided attention..."

1995
Elaine:

"It's all about power, isn't it? All the money, all the sex, it makes you feel powerful?" I huff still trying to catch my breath.

"Darling, I am powerful." He pulls me close, nibbles my ear, then lets me go. Truthfully, I'm not much of a cuddler, so I'm not upset by the abrupt end to our Sunday morning lessons.

As usual, the sex had been eye opening. Subtle, that was the way I would describe it, and wholly about my body and what would pleasure me. I think he must get off on his ability to take control and play with my body's sensations. Hence the question about money, sex, and power.

His answer is an evasion, but I don't care. He did like money and with all the money came a huge amount of power. Politicians, businessmen, banks-- they all bowed to the flow of cash. And women. We aren't exclusive.

Well, he isn't. I don't have time for another relationship in my life. Pete and his solely owned company keep me busy, it's go go go, twenty-four/seven. Once in a while I have time to work on my own projects, buying houses to flip or rent, sometimes hiring a crew to do the work. Sometimes if it's a special place, old with lots of character and charm, I like to show up and do some of the work myself. It's a rare treat that I have time to work on my houses personally. I can't wait to head home this time and see how my latest house is shaping up.

Right now, my real estate projects are small, but it's a place to start. And I want to learn how to do things the right way.

I sigh and roll over onto my stomach. Pete and I are good companions and we work well together. It's hard to spend this much time with someone and not get sick of them. But when I need time to clear my head I go home for a week and work on a project. Or, lately, plan the huge charity event for the Women's Shelter.

I want a career and he wants an assistant and we both need a friend. We're a good match. I can tell he misses his wife. She was his closest friend and no one else came close to him the way she did.

I can never compare to his late wife, I know that. Even after all these years, he still thinks of her, though he never admits it to me.

It's a simple look in the eyes, seen only by someone who spent more time with him than anyone else. Only once in a while do I notice it, when he allows himself a minute of rest.

I'm not sure if the situation were reversed, that I'd have handled the incident as well as he did. If it had been the love of my life and my child that died, torn from away in such a violent way I might have crumbled. His kid was only eight years old. It was terrible.

The phone rings, Pete grabs it since we are in his room.

I pause just long enough to know the conversation starts with "Hello" and quickly melts into another language.

Russian. So, I don't know what Pete's saying specifically, but having read the reports on the deal I know he's being thrown a pretty enticing sales pitch.

Brewster wanted Pete to talk to the client directly and get a feel for him. Pete has a good sense for people and what will motivate them. Investment overseas, especially in the oil industry, can be a risky business, but high risk means high reward. It was a new concept to me, letting your money work for you. Never letting it sit stagnant. Acquiring companies, buying stock and holding it, commercial real estate, these are the ways to make your money grow.

Growing up, my parents worked endlessly at hourly paying jobs, in order to pay the bills and put a little savings aside when possible. Their advice to me was to do the same. Only they hoped I would make more money. It seemed to me at the time a silly concept. Make money, spend most of it, stick the rest in a bank and pretend it doesn't exist. As I grew up and savings returns became smaller and smaller, I began to think about how I could invest smarter.

Squirreling away money in trash bags to sit and rot seemed safe to my parents, but in the end, it would not grow. The monetary value would always stay the same.

Didn't it make more sense to invest the money in something that would give higher returns? Most people are scared of the risk, but Pete was teaching me how to assess the risk and make smart fiscal decisions. Even so, sometimes there was a loss.

And Pete has more than enough money to risk overseas. Anyone who talks about their 'offshore accounts' has at least some money to play with.

On the other end of the spectrum, I'm just starting out. I'm lucky enough to have a great salary, so I've used my own money to start buying and flipping houses.

I don't let Pete help me, even though he's offered. I know his part would be as an investor, but it doesn't feel right. Plus, I am a little stubborn and I want to see if I can do this on my own. But you should know Pete never gives handouts.

One time his sister asked him for a hundred thousand dollars. We were at dinner. It was an awkward dinner already, but this question made it worse. We were in one of Pete's favorite restaurants. The type with white table clothes and servers in tuxes.

"What do you need the money for?" he had asked her, leaning forward elbows on the table as if he was at a business meeting, serious all at once.

I remember her looking taken aback. I must admit his presence at a conference table is much more intimidating than that of a typical dinner companion. But she was talking money, and money was his empire.

"Well," she paused, realized he was being serious and floundering to think of a response. I guess she decided to come clean and be honest. No sense in hiding, he'd find out eventually.

She took a sip of wine and started again. "Well, it would just make me feel more comfortable, having that money in the bank."

She smiled at him. Appealing to his sense of family, which, honestly, I'm not sure he has much of anymore. Ever since he lost his wife and kid, he didn't make much time for family. An obligatory dinner once or twice a year was all his sister got, their parents having passed away years ago. Usually he spends Christmas diving in the Caribbean or climbing some exotic mountain.

I'll never forget his serious face fading to a neutral place. He picked up his fork and knife and cut into his steak, medium rare. This was not, after all, a business meeting.

There was no hesitation or thinking on the matter. He did not give handouts. "If you want money, work for it, like everybody else." That settled it, and he chewed his steak. I tried not to laugh at the face she made.

Now, I am learning to make money work for me, but on a much smaller scale than Pete's. I always write out a business plan, try to think out all the possibilities of failure and how to proceed in such a situation.

For example, buy a rundown house for cash at a ridiculously reduced price. Pete always tells me cash on the table is really hard for a seller to pass up, even if you are offering half of what they wanted. Then I fix the house up a little and sell it, or if it's in the right area, and it makes sense to hold the property a while, I rent it out.

My business plan includes contingencies, like if the house doesn't rent for a few months. Would I be able to cover the taxes and upkeep? For how long? Things like that.

It's common sense really, take on a little at a time until it all adds up.

Now every month I get a couple of rent checks from tenants. It's a start.

I bounce off the bed and pull on a black lace bra and matching panties, then continue my perusal of the Sunday edition of the Wall Street Journal.

"Spasibo, Proshchay." He hangs up the phone, and heads into the restroom to take a shower. I decide to follow.

"What do you think? Was Brewster right? Can you snatch up the company?" My toothbrush is still wet from brushing right before sleep, only a couple of hours ago. A shiver runs up my spin remembering what we had done together.

His lips on my neck, his hands on me. Everywhere. I can't help but smile noticing how tender my nipples feel. I brush my fingertips over them making them react. My lips look full and red in the fogging mirror. I begin to breath faster with the memories of pleasure. He takes great pleasure in me, and I in him. My body starts waking, my skin is craving more touch.

Pete answers my business question and pulls me back to reality, "Yes, I think he's really motivated." he changes the subject suddenly. "By the way, I've got a meeting with Karen tomorrow to talk over that Apple Company."

Karen! The CEO of Money Trust!

My toothbrush still in my mouth I exclaim, "Wha!?" Apple was a company I had mentioned!

"It looks good, and I have to invest in technology sooner or later. Oil is pretty risky right now, so we are going to have to be cautious. But this computer company, I've looked it over. We could get good returns if their product does even moderately as well as you think it will. The shares are just under a dollar right now." He pokes his head out from the glass doors and smiles that enigmatic smile. I melt a little, and then spit.

He is making it hard to talk business. What with all his naked skin and the dripping water.

I'm thinking again of our twilight hours. I flashback, looking down on his torso working with mine. We looked sexy together, moving in slow deliberate rhythms.

Trying to finish the business chat quickly I step over to the shower. "I hope Karen agrees, I think it's a good bet." Then I lean forward and seek a kiss that is granted.

Enough with the business conversation-- it's Sunday, after all. Leaning against the shower frame I ask, "Can we make this shower any hotter?" It's corny. I don't care, it has the desired effect.

He lifts me effortlessly into the shower, making me feel strong and weak at the same time. How can a man like this desire me?

What a good life.

As Pete's tongue wakes all the sensitive areas on my body I moan in pleasure and anticipation.

How strange these glorious moments of respite life grants to us.

Honestly, it is sometimes hard for me to imagine all the horrible things he's gone through in his life. I've heard of the wars, the deaths, and the true heartbreak that comes with living a life as fully and passionately as possible.

"Sex is sex, love is love. They are two different god damned animals."

Pete:
1966

I have this friend who I like to think of as the sex nymph. She used to call me up with a conquest in mind. We were both married at the time, but that had nothing to do with it. This was just sex and fun.

One time, there was this gorgeous woman my nymph wanted-- let's call this other woman Grace. Well, the sex nymph, we can call her Jessica, she knew I could close a deal so to speak, so she decided I should take the two of them out to dinner. Why not, I thought.

We went to a nice restaurant just outside the city. We wined and dined. It wasn't difficult to suggest a nightcap somewhere private, and Grace's apartment was close by. My friend Jessica set on some soft music as I poured them more wine.

"Have a seat on the couch, I'll give you a massage while you sip your wine," I told Grace.

It's difficult to resist a good massage and I give a great massage. I could tell this girl wanted me, we were all in the mood and ready.

As I slowly massaged this beautiful woman's body, I began to undress her. Her soft dress was draped over the back of a chair. Then the bra followed by her silk panties. With all the fabric out of the way I found new warm and sensitive places to massage the oil, and I kissed her all over, made her hungry for it. I kissed her and used my tongue to stimulate her g- spot. I do love the sound of a beautiful lady moaning in response to my attentions. It makes me good and ready.

At some point, I turned around and undressed my friend Jessica, kissing her and fondling her similarly.

Grace was quivering at this point and ready for more. I asked her if she would please touch herself while she watched us and she gladly obliged.

I knew it was time. I lifted and placed my sex nymph down next to Grace on the couch so that the soft skin of their legs touched, and I told Grace, "Pay attention." Then I went down on my nymph.

Grace paid rapt attention, as instructed. Cupping herself with her hands and panting heavier and faster with each passing detail of my instruction.

When the Nymph could barely take more and began to moan and move against me I addressed Grace again. I pulled my head out from between Jess's legs and said, "Now you try it." Then I kissed Grace slowly so she could taste Jessica on my lips and tongue.

Grace didn't even hesitate, she was so hot and bothered. She got on her knees and stuck on like a magnet.

My nymph's eyes went round as saucers! I'll never forget her face!

I let Grace finish Jess off, and then I fucked her over the arm of the couch. She came twice before I turned to had sex with my nymph, payment and pleasure for a job well done.

I love to make women cum, it's all about the G- spot. The "good spot" my friend Annie used to call it. Oh god, let me tell you about Miss Annie, that woman taught me all about the good spot.

"I think she had about seven diamond rings."

Spring 1957
Pete

When I was seventeen I met Miss Annie. She ruined most men. She'd been engaged at least seven times. She would sex them, throw them around and then it would be over. At thirty-one years of age she was still beautiful, with a model's body, long legs and smooth skin that went on forever. She also had perfect breasts.

Miss Annie was big in New York; she might have been a call girl, I never asked. I know she had her own money. In the summer she would come back home to see her parents and the teenage kid she always introduced as her brother. But I knew better. She was probably about fifteen when he was born.

It was in early May when Annie showed up. It was a crazy day for sure. Not only did I meet Annie, but Jimmy shot himself and I laid eyes on my future wife for the first time.

Swim practice got out around 3:30. The guys always hung around after practice, but I usually had somewhere else to be.

"Hey Niner, have a good weekend!"

"Yeah, good practice, see you Monday," I called, heading for the showers. I needed to hurry. I wanted to check on one of my house sites. The walls were going up on my fifth house. It was slower during the school year, but once summer hit I was sure we could build faster.

"Pete, you gonna head down to Raymond's place later?"

Raymond's was the drive-in diner and creamery in town. It was one of the local hang outs. I would often take my Harley there in the evenings.

"Maybe later. I promised Jimmy I'd go see that new pistol."

"Alright, just watch yourself. You know how well Jim aims!" The guys all had a good laugh.

My cousin Jimmy had been talking about his new Ruger single six .22 caliber all week. He insisted that he could draw and fire faster than any of us now, and I was keen to see if it was true since I highly doubted the claim.

I finished up and put on my jeans and white shirt and leather jacket. Mr. Burt had given it to me when I bought and fixed up my first Harley. It was black leather, with a skull and crossbones on the back. I liked the way it made people eye me, as if they didn't know whether or not I was dangerous. I wasn't in a biker gang, but no one else knew that.

The synchronized swimming teams were entering as I made my way out. I slowed down a bit to enjoy the view. Twenty young women strutting by me wearing next to nothing.

Some glanced at me in passing, others were embarrassed and pretended I wasn't there by averting their eyes, but one girl looked directly at me and smiled a big knowing smile.

She was gorgeous. Big blue eyes, pale clear skin, dark auburn colored hair, and a fit athletic body with just the right amount of curves. I caught myself wondering what was she smiling about? Also what school was she from? Maybe she liked motorcycles? I could take her for a ride. I winked at her. To my surprise, she kept smiling and winked back. How bold! Then she dove in the pool.

My first stop was to my building site. A single-family house on a two-acre plot of land. The house looked good, coming along on schedule. The siding was up, the roof was done and the electrical and plumbing were almost in. I would stop by over the weekend to help with the interior walls. It was close to the end of the work day so I handed out the paychecks and let the crew head home.

Then I rode my motorcycle out to Jimmy's family farm on the edge of town, a sprawling property with an old farmhouse set at the end of a long driveway. The guys were already outside when I pulled up. The roar of my Harley died out and they walked over.

"I figured we could shoot over in the cornfield." Jimmy already had the Ruger holstered to his side.

The field had recently been plowed and was ready for planting. Jimmy drew his gun and fired. I remember the little puffs of dust floating up as the bullets hit the ground. He actually could draw pretty fast.

With a gun like this you've got to cock the pistol while you're drawing it. Well, after a couple shots the god damn thing went off while he was drawing.

Me and the guys looked around for a bit looking for the bullet before Jimmy put his hand on his knee and said, "Ow, jeez, my knee hurts."

I looked down and saw blood spreading, so I said, "Drop your pants." It was like someone took a black pencil and drew a line down his leg.

"Jimmy, my friend--" I was trying not to laugh. "You've shot yourself!"

The bullet had settled on his knee and was resting right between the skin and his kneecap.

"It went in and it never came out!" our buddy Lou exclaimed.

I could have cut it right out with my knife. But I didn't. We had to take him to the hospital, and the cops have to come when there's a gunshot wound so that's how the local newspaper found out.

The headline the next day was amazing! It read:

"The Lamb was playing Lion and Shot Himself, and now he's going back to Tiddlywinks."

I started calling him Wyatt Earp after that day. I was the only one who could get away with it. Everyone else got their asses beat if they tried.

God, Jimmy's mom was pissed!

We got him bandaged up and then decided to beat the evening heat down at the Raymond's Place with some ice cream. We were all having a good laugh at Jimmy's expense when Annie happened.

She walked right up to me with her impossibly long legs, made even longer by the white shorts she seemed to have painted onto her body. I was leaning on my motorcycle watching her, not caring that she saw me watching. Any women who dressed like that wanted to be seen, and I wasn't a shy boy.

Her hair was pulled off her face; she had just the right amount of makeup on, highlighting her cheekbones and long lashes. Most guys probably thought she wasn't wearing any.

I have an eye for little details. Like the fact that her sleeveless button up flannel was tied just high enough so that the skin of her belly showed with every hip swaying step. I liked that detail, and she knew it.

When my gaze finally made it up her curving body to her brown eyes, I thought about how she was gonna be trouble. And I couldn't wait.

Without hesitation, she said, "Take me for a ride." Who would say no to her? I tell you, nobody! I left my buddies in a heartbeat. Lou was laughing like mad while Jimmy tried to look offended. But I knew anyone of them would have done the same.

Off we went leaving a trail of dust.

I always had two saddlebags on my motorcycle that held my survival kit, consisting of one blanket and one pillow. We had sex that first night in a secluded field under the stars.

She was the one who taught me how to please a woman.

I had been having sex for nearly three years at this point, with girls from around town and girls from school, but Annie was different. She was a woman. She had experience and confidence. Maybe that's something she saw in me as well, self-assurance. I was always comfortable with myself-- I could fight and I could fuck. A fight was never something I looked forward to, but being with a woman was my favorite pastime. I never did things I wasn't good at, but Annie showed me more about a woman's body than was right for any teenager to know.

For one thing, she was the first women I ever saw with a shaved pussy. It took me by surprise that first night, but I soon knew why she preferred it that way. Smooth and clean. She taught me all about oral sex and the G spot.

After Annie, when I would find the g spot, women would often say to me, "I've only read about that in books!" And I would respond, "Well now you know it's true."

One night that summer Annie came by my house. "Pete!" My dad yelled up the stairs to me. "You've got company!"

It was already dark outside. My younger sister was across the hall from me doing her homework, her curlers already set in her hair for the night. She looked up as I stood at the landing and heard my mother ask from below, "Who is it?"

"It's a friend of Peter's who needs his help." My father was being cryptic. I hit the bottom of the stairs and turned into the kitchen as my mother retreated into the family room, not wanting to be seen in her house coat.

Standing just outside the door was Miss Annie. She had on a summer halter dress that showed off her slender arms and an ample amount of her chest.

"See ya, Pete." Dad was sarcastic as I ignored him, making straight for the door. I turned back and smiled at him.

"Be back late," I let him know, and God, I could tell my dad was envious. He shook his head and I knew what he was thinking. How the heck does a seventeen-year-old kid get a girl like that?

I would joke that it was the Harley, but the real reason was between me and Annie. We had a mutual respect for one another, and while I learned from her the many ways to please a woman, she got what she needed, too. I think she gained some pleasure from being my teacher.

She looked sexy straddling my bike wearing that dress. So many times we got on my bike and found a new place to spend the night. Annie and I weren't in a relationship, we were just fucking. We both knew that without having to talk about it.

On mornings after my nights with Annie I always allowed myself a bit of a late start. This was because I liked to lay around watching her morning ritual: a breast massage.

Yup, every single morning Miss Annie would get up early, stand in front of the mirror naked, and work on her breasts. It always made me want her, but usually I would let her finish her exercise first. She believed massage kept her breasts firm and young looking. She had fantastic breasts so I guess she was right. Watching her beautiful body from behind as she lifted, pushed and oiled her flesh, I figured I had the best seat in the house.

But that day Jimmy shot himself, even after meeting Annie, I couldn't help but think about the bold girl I had seen at the pool. Lying in bed late that night I thought, "how funny to be thinking of the girl from the synchronized swim team when I can still smell Annie on me.

Eventually I had to give in and admit I couldn't get that other girl out of my head, which of course meant I needed to find out who she was.

Barbara:

I had seen her, of course, and I had thought of her. Usually, I was the one who made the first move. But with Barbara everything was different.

It was April of 1957 when we finally met. I was seventeen years old and she was fifteen.

Jimmy, my cousin, otherwise known as Wyatt Earp, was actually going out with Barb's girlfriend Nancy. What a small world!

Jim and I share the same aunt and uncle by marriage, him on the uncle side and me on the aunt side. I guess that means we aren't technically cousins, but we might as well have been. We were both into Harley Davidson motorcycles so we used to hang around at the shop or in my dad's garage.

One day Nancy, Jim's girlfriend, accompanied him to the shop. He wanted to tinker on his bike. She had come with a different mission.

"Peter, you caught the eye of my friend. She wants to know if we could have a double date?"

I pulled a face. A double date sounded boring. "I don't know, Nance." I handed Jim a wrench and he returned my face. He wasn't too keen on a double either. Little chance to get alone time.

"She's real pretty," she coaxed. "Athletic, too. She's in the Dolphin Club."

"Dolphin Club?" I wondered. Could it be her?

"She says you've smiled at her once after your swim practice." Nancy smiled, seeming to know my inner thoughts. Could she really be talking about the girl I couldn't shake, the one that kept jumping into my thoughts at random?

"Nancy," I said, "do you mean that beautiful girl that does the precision swimming, big blue eyes, gorgeous smile?"

She laughed. "You've described half the team, but that sounds like Barbara."

"Barbara." I repeated the name. "Why do you think she may be interested in going out with me?" I asked. Jimmy groped for a socket wrench, but I ignored him.

"Pete!"

"Aw, sorry Jimmy." I handed him the wrong size and he sighed and got up to find it himself.

"Leave it to you. Only sidetracked by a woman." He knelt back down to continue his work, laughing at my expense.

"Peter," Nancy said, "Half the girls in school would like to date you." Jimmy looked up at her annoyed, was she one of those girls? Nancy stuck her tongue out at him.

"Why?" I teased. "I am a bad boy and she seems like a nice girl."

"You've answered your own question. Maybe she wants a bad boy. You have quite the reputation." Her smile was telling.

"Alright, Nance, I'll try this double date."

The next day, Nancy introduced me to Barbara and I liked her immediately. I asked her out for Saturday night to double date with Nancy and Jim. We went to the drive-in, also known as the "Passion Pit".

It was a little too cramped in the car with the others so Barb and I went for a walk not caring much about the movie. She was clever and funny. We talked about math and I told her about my business. She seemed impressed and mentioned how she'd love to see one of my houses.

We really did hit it off. I had never seen anyone so lovely. She wore her hair longer than most girls at the time. I liked that she wasn't afraid to be a little different.

I caught myself examining the uniqueness of her features. Her strong jaw. Glossy thick lashes framing her crystal blue eyes. The lines of muscle on her neck, and in her legs. She was an athlete after all. I wanted so badly to feel where the hardness gave way to soft, to explore her loveliness.

We walked along the line of the woods far enough so the cars and movie were left behind. In the moonlight the deep red of her hair shown like embers in a fire, to me she was the most beautiful person I'd ever seen.

I had a mustache in those days and most girls wanted to kiss me to see what it felt like. Barbara was no exception and she let me kiss her. I had kissed many girls, and most were terribly inexperienced.

Barb's inexperience meant nothing, because she and I enjoyed the best kiss I'd ever had, and honestly ever would.

She was perfect, lips soft and attentive. She was assertive but not overly aggressive. It was like Goldilocks and her porridge-- too hot, too cold, and I had found just right.

Boy, I was hooked. I'll never remember what the movie was that night, but I do remember the kisses. We did not fool around at all that night, just kissed. I don't know why I didn't take it farther; I could tell she wanted to. Maybe some other part of me understood this girl was different, special. Don't ask me why. I'd never thought that before, and I've never thought it since!

I got her home before midnight. "Can I see you again soon?" She looked so hopeful, and I have to admit the idea of spending more time with her made me excited.

"Certainly," I told her happily.

She got up on her tiptoes and kissed me once more.

"Tomorrow?" I asked eagerly, and she laughed before going inside closing the door without giving an answer. She was certainly something special.

I wanted to see her all the time after that, but her parents only let her go out once a week, so I asked her out for the next Saturday night. I had made an okay impression on them. After all I was on the honor roll and had my own business. Her dad was a tool designer and her mom a registered nurse. They were good hardworking people, my kind of people.

That Saturday eventually came but it seemed like ages.

I really wanted to impress Barbara's father and mother, a feeling that had never occurred to me with any other girl I had taken out.

I had a new pickup truck which I used for my business, and they didn't know I owned a motorcycle, too. Of course, I picked her up in my truck, thinking it would look better than if I pulled up wearing a skull and crossbones jacket on a Harley. I took her for dinner first, before returning again to the Passion Pit.

She smelled so good. No perfume, just rose soap with an underlying fragrance unique only to her.

Barb never wore much makeup. That night, our first night on our own she had on just a bit of lipstick, to show off her beautifully soft, kissable lips.

Ignoring the movie once more, we started kissing. To hell with the movie. This girl seemed to infect my brain. "Barb," I told her, "I've never enjoyed making out with someone this much in my whole life." And I meant it. To this day I've never kissed another woman and felt that way.

"I feel the same." She smiled. "Though from what I hear, I don't have your kind of experience."
She wasn't acting jealous, just joking around. I liked that, so I went in for more.

Her sweater was unbuttoned halfway so I reached over and began stroking her breasts. Her nipples hardened when I squeezed them gently, and she stopped kissing me long enough to gasp, "Peter, I have never let anyone touch me before."

She wasn't saying to stop; in fact, she was becoming excited. She kissed me more and pressed herself against me.

I kissed her again and again. Her lips and tongue were amazing things to bite and explore. But never wanted her to regret anything so I stopped at one point to say, "Listen, we'd better slow down, baby, or your panties will be down around your ankles."

She used no words to respond, just her confident laughter and her firm grip. I came up for breath one more time. "There will be no turning back."

She broke her silence and gave me her concise answer which left nothing to question: "I've got to lose my virginity sometime and I am more than ready now."

That was all the invitation I needed. Both her panties and my pants were well past our ankles before long. She wanted to lose her virginity and I wanted to take it. We were a match made in heaven.

"I like to win. You know second is just another way to say first loser."

January 1958
Pete:

My last two years of high school were busy years. I had plenty of girls to chase and a growing business. I still played baseball. During my last year, I was even being looked at for a pro team. I had a fast arm and twenty-ten vision, so the scouts were at my games.

It seemed I was on my way to a big bold life that people would envy, but in the end my future would be rather anonymous. I guess things really changed for me in the Navy.

I was picked out especially for my diving and athleticism. But when the training was over I was informed that my position on the sub would be a front. I was to wear neither dog tags nor mark my body with tattoos of any kind. Secrets abounded at the time, it was the cold war and we had a Nation to protect. Eventually my clearance in the military became top secret. Obscurity was something I perfected in the Navy, but it was in the civilian world when anonymity became a crucial part of my life.

Over the years my father maintained a position in the Navy. On my seventeenth birthday, he was on shore duty stationed at the reserve center, so he brought me over and had me sign up for Navy Reserve duty. There's a part of me that thinks he wanted to keep me out of trouble. Nothing, not even the Navy, could protect me from that.

Being in the Navy reserves means serving at least two years' active duty. I served six years' total, four years in the reserve and two years on active duty.

I had money saved up and could have gone to college, but at the time, being a submarine sailor was a very special thing, and it was something I had prepared for my whole life. All the years of training my father had put me through had set me up for this very specific type of service. Not many people were accomplished divers-- it was a rare talent.

Serving on a sub is much different than other types of Naval service. Every bit of space is valuable, equating to a very austere lifestyle.

It's probably one of the reasons my wife and I never fought. I always kept my clothing folded neat and tucked out of the way, and I always picked my socks up. I've heard so many women bitching about how their men don't clean up after themselves and it always makes me shake my head. What a silly thing to waste time arguing over. Barb and I always had better things to do. Socks are just socks, and they aren't hard to keep track of.

On a sub, we needed room for more than just the men, and their clothing. Food for example. Finding room for so many months of food supply was part of my job. I used to store cases of canned goods lining the passageways. We would just walk right on over them.

If you've never been on a sub it's probably hard to imagine living in such close quarters. During war time a sailor often didn't get his own bunk, that's how tight space was. While I served, we weren't at war. Which meant I at least had my own bed. However, I had heard it described, "hot bunking". Two or three sailors would be assigned the same bunk, and they would sleep in shifts. When one sailor finished his shift of work he would head off to sleep only to find it was still "hot" from the sailor who had just woken up. Yeah, it was tight.

Even so I loved being at sea.

For three months at a time, my home was a submarine. A guppy they called it. Unlike the World War Two fleet boats, a guppy could use a snorkel to expel the exhaust of the diesel engines and take in fresh air. This way we hardly ever surfaced. We could live for the most part under water. It's never quite comfortable, always a little oppressive and cramped, but a person can get used to pretty much anything if they are tough enough and don't give up.

According to all the records I was a cook. Don't get me wrong, I really did cook. Every three days I had a shift preparing food for the crew.

But cooking wasn't why I joined the Navy-- by the time most kids were just learning to swim I was a master diver and my superiors knew it. Since we would spend three months mostly submerged, the ship needed someone who could recover torpedoes or fix the exterior of the sub while it was still under water. Sometimes my dive would entail other more serious and secretive reasons.

My job in the galley was a front, not necessarily to my crew members, but on the record. Nowhere is it written that part of my job was to swim around in the deep black waters of the North Atlantic Ocean and tap enemy communication lines, or deal with any other aspects of our covert operations. The truth was my main purpose on the boat was to be the diver.

Once I was asked to save the boat by performing a rather tricky dive. It was early July of 1958, I was eighteen years old.

"Pete, we need you to take a swim," the Chief told me. He was the COB, Chief of the Boat, but we shortened it to just Chief. On a boat there's the Captain, and then there's the COB. He's God's right hand man. On a submarine the Captain is God. You ever go on a sub he's the closest to God you'll ever get. The Chief was in charge of us men, and you didn't keep him waiting, especially when he says we are in enough danger to send a diver, like me, out for a swim.

There I was hunkered down for some sleep, having just read a nice letter from Barbara. She was a sweet little thing, saying she missed me and wanted to see me during my next leave. I knew how bold she had been to write it. She was a shy girl, but that became a little less apparent when she spent time with me, and I liked the change I made in her. Yes, I wanted to see her. I decided when I got back to dry land I would drive home and pick her up on my Harley, and show her a nice time.

I was already swinging out of my cramped bunk when I addressed the chief. "What seems to be the problem, Chief?" He fell in step behind me as we ducked through a hatch feet first on our way to the forward torpedo room.

"We're stuck."

Trapped, I thought. Trapped at sixty feet, in enemy water. "Stuck?"

"On the nets."

Ah, the nets, I nodded my head thinking about our situation, taking a second to formulate a basic plan.

We were running a series of covert operations in enemy waters, deep in the North Atlantic. For instance, communication cables had been run along the bottom of the ocean so our enemy could communicate along vast distances. There were no such things as satellite communication at the time. It was our job to find these cables, tap into them, and have a direct link to their conversations. In this way, we could learn about possible attacks and in general keep track of any enemy advancement in technology or weaponry.

One way in which our crafty opposition tried to deter such missions was by surrounding their harbors with steel netting. Simple but effective.

On that particular day we had been trying to sneak right into an enemy harbor. Ballsy, I know!

Unfortunately, our boat had got caught up on one of these harbor nets and now we were stuck like one big fish. It was only a matter of time before we were discovered and blown to smithereens.

"We need you to cut us loose so we can go about our mission unnoticed."

There's very little joking in a situation like this. We were in trouble. The chief didn't need to remind me that the life of the crew was in my hands.

We both nodded at one another as the chief went back to the control room and I started to prepare myself for the dive.

My gear consisted of the lined pants and trousers that made up foul weather gear and a dry suit directly over it, all of this in an attempt to insulate my body from the cold. But it was cold enough that a diver only had a few minutes to work before hypothermia set in.

My dive belt held a knife and a flashlight. Everything was strapped to me in case it was dropped, because if you dropped that flashlight you were fucked. With no light I couldn't find my way to the snag in order to save the boat and of course the crew.

It's dark in the North Atlantic, where we ran the majority of our missions. Some places in the world the ocean is crystal clear, a tropical paradise like in the Caribbean. But the waters up north, they aren't clear or warm. It was technically summer the day I took that fateful dive, but I knew the water outside was going to be dark as night after fifteen feet and cold as death.

On this trip, I also tied a portable saw to me. I climbed into the forward escape hatch and waited. You can't just open a hatch on a submerged boat, you have to bleed in the air and make the pressure in the chamber the same as the pressure outside the sub before the hatch will open. It's pretty quick for it to fill with water. You kind of do it all at the same time. It took several minutes of just waiting while the freezing water filled and the pressure equalized. We were in about sixty feet of water. Six tenths times forty-four point four means about twenty-seven pounds per square inch. That would do it. I could then just open the hatch and swim out. No big deal, for me.

I guess it might be a big deal for someone unaccustomed to diving into the weighted pressure of the vast ocean and having the pitch-black envelope them. To me it felt almost comforting, as if all the distraction and noise of everyday life had just been turned off like a light switch.

Before getting to work on the nets I had to attach a line from myself to the hatch, and then the hatch has to be closed and dogged. A quick couple of spins and it's all set. Now the boat is secure; they can run and leave me behind if they have to.

The reason I never had a set of dog tags, and was one of the only sailors on the boat with no tattoos was to protect our ultimate mission. It was how it had to be for men like me. We had high security clearance and the understanding that if our bodies went missing no one was going to try to find us. We would be unmarked and unidentifiable. Therefore, if my body was ever recovered by the enemy, they wouldn't be able to tell who I was or where

I was from. I could have been anyone, not necessarily from the United States at all.

We weren't supposed to be out there doing what we were doing. We were to speak of our actions with no one.

When your life is possibly on the line, and you are all on your own with what seems like the pressure of the whole ocean on you, it's hard not to reflect on your life a little. That day I thought of everyone back home and what they would do if I went missing. They wouldn't get a body or even a real explanation. Just that I had died in service.

How devastated my mom would be! My dad, he would be sad but proud that I served my country. Then I thought of Barbara. Would she miss me? Not for long. She was young and incredibly smart, and strong. She would get snatched up, marry young. Would another man see her, really see how incredibly unique she was? This train of thought upset me.

Wait! What the fuck was I doing? Getting caught up on such thoughts when I was sixty feet underwater in the midnight blackness, wanting to shiver in the cold, while I had a job to do. I had to focus! Damn stupid time to be thinking like that. I cleared my mind and got to work.

Sure enough, the starboard bow plane was caught in a steel net. It was quick work with the portable saw to free us up, only about a minute or so. But when I turned to go back home there were a pair of divers coming down to see what the hell was going on. My asshole was up in my throat and I knew I was in deep shit.

I shut my light off so they couldn't see me. A flashlight at that depth is like a beacon bright as the sun. But it travels in glaring shafts, and doesn't light much up around it. It was in this way I managed to keep track of the two divers. They didn't turn their lights off.

They were searching for something but they didn't know yet that it was a boat. They didn't know I was there yet; they just wanted to see what was stuck on their nets.

Well, I wasn't gonna let them find me first. I had the upper hand since I could see them; they were looking into an ocean of darkness. Quick as possible, I made my move on the first diver. Springing up off the metal beneath my feet, I let the water flow over me as I twisted in the water. The slightest of movements coming from my hips, set me up to float undetected around to his back. It took only seconds, and he was dead, just like that. From behind him I reached up with my knife in hand and cut his airline.

The second diver had of course seen me at this point. He slashed at my leg, but I ignored his clumsy advance and reached out to cut the tube supplying his air too.

It made the most sense. Why try to stab him, when slicing through one line in one sure movement could finish him off instantly?

These divers had on weights in order to help them sink faster on their dive. These weights would give us a little more time to escape, because their bodies wouldn't surface.

I watched for a second as both men sank deeper into the dark abyss and disappeared. There's no way to know how long it took those two men to die. It could have been minutes or maybe much longer depending on their lung capacity and the amount of oxygen in their blood. Either way it's a pretty terrible way to die.

But I couldn't pause to think about them. I hightailed it twenty feet back to the escape hatch. No time to think. Time was running out.

I was in a hurry for a couple of reasons, one because it was so cold, and secondly because when the guys up top figured out their men weren't going to resurface we would be barraged with depth charges, and it would all be over.

As soon as the water level in the hatch lowered below the 1MC radio, I stuck my face right up to it to let the Captain know we had to run. The 1MC is an intercom system throughout the boat. You just hit the button and talk. It's at the top of the hatch, so I only needed a couple of inches to drain before I could shout into it.

I remember being out of breath as I shouted, "Get the hell out of here. Go fast and go quiet!" The water drains down into the bilges of the sub. Once that water is out I can go down into the sub. It wasn't until I was back in the warm of the ship, peeling off my suit, that I realized the gash in my thigh. That was gonna leave a nasty scar for sure.

Well, that message got the Captain's attention. He wanted to see me right away. Sonar wasn't great back then, but it was good enough that they could tell something more than cutting nets had happened.

He asked for my verbal report. I kept it simple: "I cut the net, and now we gotta get the hell out of here. They know we are here."

"Well, you're bleeding pretty bad, can you explain that?"

"I got cut." The captain wasn't a stupid man. He knew I was purposefully being vague. But he decided at that point I was bleeding too much to continue our conversation. He relented for the time being.

"Go and have the corpsman take a look at your leg."

The corpsmen were like registered nurses. We didn't have doctors on board.

The corpsman wasn't so stupid either and wanted to hear the tale. "You didn't get cut on no fucking net, you got sliced."

But I had decided by then that no one would know. I told him plain and simple: "Doc, bandage me up." And that was it. Well he had to do it, and I think he took some pity on me. After all, I had just killed two men on the bottom of the sea and hadn't even paused to think about it. It was instinct, fast and cruel, but I'd do it again in an instant to save my own neck and my shipmates.

He said, "You are shaking like a leaf."

"It's cold out there," I said defensively. But it was probably nerves.

He seemed to figure the same thing and gave me some brandy.

Once I was bandaged up, it was back to the Captain's stateroom. He wasn't going to give up that easy.

He sat staring at me tried to be stern. "Tell me what really happened."

"You don't want to know, sir."

"I have to know." He was right. The Captain was God, but I didn't feel right telling him. If anyone found out about our mistake with the nets there would be repercussions. Remember when I said, we weren't supposed to be out there. We were exploring and looking for information. Information on the size of the enemy fleet, information by way of communication, but we were sort of on our own. Entering the harbor had been a calculated risk that hadn't worked out. Well, I didn't want the Captain to get into trouble.

"No sir, if you don't know, nobody can make you tell."

He relented to my subtle advice. "I shouldn't, but I will take your advice and leave it at that." It's because we weren't supposed to be there. We all knew that. We were spying. I always wondered what the guys at the harbor did when those two men never surfaced, but we were too far away by then to ever know.

Yeah, that was a close call for sure. I remember it leaning back in my rack shortly after. The close call on my mind and brandy on my breath. I allowed myself to finally reflect on my earlier thoughts of Barbara. So, I didn't want any other man to have her. That was a new one. It had never bothered me when Mary had been with others, or Miss Annie. This girl Barb, she was something special to me, all right.

"I've probably told you more about myself than anyone else, ever."

1995
Elaine:

The phone rings.
"Hello, Elaine speaking."
"Elaine, hi, it's Eddie."
Eddie if you remember, is the CEO of RICHCO's transportation and shipping branch, Get There. I knew in a second why he was calling, and was immediately annoyed.

God knows the man has better things to do. And so do I. This guy knows the transportation and shipping business like no other person. If it moves, Eddie knows about it. We've got ships, planes, trains, and trucks everywhere, so I know he's plenty busy. Who knows, maybe he just likes to end his week by harassing me. This is an old argument, so I try to preempt him.

"Mr. Wong, don't worry, everything is all set for Mr. Pete's flight tomorrow."

"All set!" His voice was a barely controlled falsetto. "All set? Elaine, come on! I've got the owner of a multibillion dollar transportation company flying tomorrow on a commercial jet!"

No matter how rich he gets Pete doesn't like to make a big deal out of traveling, which is why I usually try to keep our travel plans low key. We fly first class in great comfort and nobody even knows they are sitting next to one of the richest men in the world. Peter gets a real kick out of it.

"Eddie." We don't have to be formal; Eddie and I are really getting to be good friends. "I am much too busy to have this conversation with you again. Do you want me to transfer you to Pete's phone?"

"What?" He's shocked at my ruthlessness. "No! I don't want to bother him. And I already know he doesn't like the waste of flying the private jets!"

"I know, dear, that's why I can't for the life of me figure out why you always bug me about it." I'm all sugar and spice.

"Elaine, so help me God, I'm going to delay that plane just so he has no choice but to take the private flight."

"No you won't, Eddie, because we have hundreds of customers flying the jet that day as well. Don't mess with the customers." He makes an indignant sound on the other end. Laughing I tell him, "Calm down, it's nearly five o'clock there right? Why don't you have a gin and tonic and try to relax."

I really hope this is the last time we need to have this conversation, and I try to appease him by reminding him Pete does occasionally indulged in the pleasures wealth can bring. "Actually, I could really use some help-- I'm so swamped over here."

"Transportation or shipping related?" Eddie sounds intrigued.

"Sort of. It's about Pete's catamaran."

"I'm listening." Eddie was currently in the Caribbean at one of our other bases of operation. Peter once owned a huge chunk of real estate there which he had parceled off in small lots for millions. Now he had a tasteful beach house on a private stretch of beach and an office complex that stood to represent the oil and gasoline aspect of his empire. Eddie liked to stay on the island while it was cold and wintery back home.

"Since you are already on Saint Eustatius, can you make sure the boat is ready? Not you personally, just ask someone on staff to look after it. I know it's a small thing, but I'm not on the island and just want to be sure she's all cleaned and ready to go for when we arrive."

"You're trying to appease me, aren't you?" But Eddie knows how much Pete loves that boat, so he's happy to help. "You know, Pete's lucky to have you, Elaine. You seem to understand him so well."

After fifteen years, I'm sure Eddie would like to know more about his boss, that's for sure, but he'll get nothing but the cheerful jokester. I get the serious guy with all the war stories and memories.

I sigh. "Yes, well, aren't we all lucky. And Eddie?"

"Yes, Elaine?"

"Don't you even think about calling me next week when we fly down to join you. We are flying commercial from JFK, it's only got one stop and he's perfectly happy about it."

"God! Pete with a layover." He's closer to joking now. "I give up, you two can fly at the back of the plane for all I care!"

"Thanks, Mr. Wong, but that won't be necessary." Amused sarcasm laces my every word.

"Fly safe, dear, I'll see you in a week." We are friends once more.

"Have a gin and tonic waiting for me!"

"Will do." His end goes dead.

It seems strange. Fifteen years is a long time to be acquainted with someone but not really know them. I have noticed Pete just doesn't have close friends, and he is private to the point of paranoia.

But he talks to me, and I don't know why. He says it to me all the time: "You know more about my life than anyone else," and that I'm so easy to talk to. He has plenty of sex with other women, but they don't get his stories.

Some of his tall tales are just funny pieces of his life, like how he got transferred to another submarine after some lady hung her panties in a tree.

Other stories seem as if they come from a Hollywood film. Like the one time he dove off a surfaced submarine to rescue a civilian woman who had fallen off.

He tells me they were on the Saint Lawrence River in Alexandria, New York, celebrating the completion of the locks system the United States and Canada had just built on the river. He was nineteen I think, so that would make it the summer of 1959.

The locks would allow ships to get from the Great Lakes to the Atlantic Ocean. The Navy had been invited to attend the festivities and the locals could tour all the submarines and ships.

Peter tells me the place was called Alexandria Bay. The people taking the tour of Pete's sub would come in and go down one hatch, tour, and come up the other end. On the older subs there wasn't a lot of room between the sail, and it gets slick from the water spraying up as the sub moved on the waves.

That's how the woman fell off the boat. She stepped wrong and slid down the side bouncing off the tanks. If it was the fifties she was probably dressed to the nines instead of in something sensible like a pair of sneakers.

The seaway was running at a swift current and Pete had been worried the woman was knocked out from bouncing off the side of the submarine.

He recounts the story lazily, like it was no big deal. "And so I just ran and jumped shoes and all."

He yelled, "Throw me a life preserver!" and ran as far as he could on the sub before jumping in.

"Of course, then there were pictures in the paper," he tells me, and then waves off the praise I try to lavish on him, saying, "Aw, someone else would have jumped in after her."

My skeptical side highly doubts that. Sure, someone might have jumped in eventually, but he dives in head first. Acting on instinct and years of intense training, trusting he could physically accomplish the deed, he saved that girl's life.

Some of his stories are much more serious. I know he's a dangerous man. Don't get me wrong, he's a good man and I trust him more than any other person, but his strong sense of justice sometimes worries me. Well, self-preservation plays a factor as well. But mostly it's his idea of justice.

After he was done with the Navy he and his wife started a shelter for battered women and children. That's why we are heading back to the States in a day, to attend the annual banquet that raises money for the shelter and the fund attached to it.

Pete is still intimately involved with the shelter and tells me frequently how much he dislikes it when a man beats on a woman. "It just makes no sense," he always says. "I'm not trying to offend you, Elaine, but for the most part women are smaller and men are so much stronger."

I tend to agree with him. I've seen him in the boxing ring and I know what a man's fist can do. Whatever the reason for this level of candor, I am happy to be the recipient of these stories.

He jokes around a lot and says, "Honey, only I know what is true and what isn't," but I'd like to think I can tell the difference. Even if he always tells me he's a dirty old man, which I know to be true, I also believe him to be good.

The shelter project, for instance. As a young married couple, Peter and Barbara lived in a poor area, and too often they would see domestic abuse happening to innocent kids and women.

As usual, my dear boss couldn't stand to wait for the legal system to react in its slow fashion. He dove in head first. He would get them somewhere safe, and then he would send in the cavalry. I don't know if Barb knew about the latter.

Pete had this friend who had been adopted as a kid. Before his parents adopted him, he spent some time in the system. It's not a great system now, and it was worse then. Needless to say, it was a rough upbringing and he had a sore spot when it came to people abusing children and women.

So, if a little kid came to them with broken bones and bruises all over this "friend" of Pete's would be sent to find the father or stepfather who had done the beating. Peter told me very matter-of-factly one afternoon, "I figured if they knew what it felt like to have someone snap their own arm like that, well then, they'd think twice about doing it again."

I trust Peter with my life, that's for sure. I'm on his team, and we have a special bond. He would protect me at any cost. But heaven help those sorry sons of bitches who think they can get away with harming someone innocent. They've got another thing coming.

"A secret is a secret only if one person knows it."

Pete:

I never saw a woman that I really wanted that I couldn't get. When I used to go away for real estate conferences I would fuck around. That's how it was with the conferences, and it made perfect sense. We were staying in hotels after all. We would hook up then head home, and nobody needed to know about it. I never told my wife, and my wife never asked. It worked out perfectly.

There was one woman I met who had served in the Israeli army for a time. This is customary. A person born in Israel will often return to serve even if they were raised in another country like the United States. Both men and women serve in the army for at least one year when they reach legal adulthood.

After the military, she told me that she dabbled in acting. I don't know if she was any good at it, because by the time I met her she was a very successful real estate broker.

We met at a conference in Vegas. After a long day sitting through the conference, a bunch of us agents went out dancing. Boy, could that woman dance! I saw her hips moving and just knew I had to take her to bed.

We were only there for the weekend, so the wedding rings came off. It was lectures all day and a whole lot of fucking at night.

When we were alone in her hotel room, she said to me, "I never had sex with a Gentile before."

Always, I try to make a lovely woman laugh, so I joked with her, "Well, I'm half Jewish."

She pulled away from me looking confused. "How so?" She had an accent. It was sexy.

"I'm circumcised."

I got my laugh. "Close enough," she whispered, and then she bit my lip, which made it necessary to carry her to bed. It was a good night. We usually reenacted the scene if we met up at other conferences.

It's probably apparent, I especially like to seduce married women. This is because they know how to be discreet. I know how to be discreet as well. I don't want them in trouble and I don't want to get shot either. I learned my lesson just after I joined the Navy.

Whenever we got back to base after a few months out to sea there would be a big party. In the summer months, it was always a picnic, and all the Navy men would bring their girls. There would be food and drink to show appreciation of our service.

On one such occasion, in late July 1958 after our getting caught in the net we returned to the base and went into drydock for repairs.

This was right before I was married.

At this particular "ships picnic" I got talking to a young lady who said she had recently divorced a submariner. Then she says to me, "I want to take a ride on your motorcycle."

It was apparent that she wanted more than that, too, which made me agree all the more.

We went for a ride, and we stopped to have sex. I chose a spot just off base. We pulled over and did it right on the side of the road, near a little pond where the trees were just thick enough to hide what we were doing from passers-by.

I told her, "I've decided to make a Harley girl out of you." She didn't know what that meant so I showed her rather than explaining it. I bent her over the leather seat of my bike and took her from behind, with one hand pulling at her hair and one massaging her clit. She became a Harley girl good and quick.

I remember she left her panties hanging on the branch of a bush on the side of the road before we pulled away. I thought it was pretty hilarious at the time.

Until we got back to the picnic, that is. When we got back from the ride she found a group of her friends and she started telling them all about how we had just had sex. She was being loud on purpose. Come to find out, she was very newly divorced. I never asked why she really did it, but thinking back on it now she must have been trying to make her old man jealous.

It worked all right. He came at me, said he was gonna kill me. The chief of the boat just barely gets me away and yells at me, "What were you thinking, fucking his wife?"

"Wife! She told me they were divorced!"

"Even so, he still thinks of her as his wife."

"That's just a misunderstanding then, I can explain it to him." I didn't see what the big deal was. They were no longer married; did he think a woman like that was going to stop having sex just because she had no ring? People who think that way are crazy. Sex is an awesome thing and once you get a taste for it there's nothing that's going to stop you from getting more. I knew that, she knew that, and it would be better if the rest of the tight-assed world would figure it out as well.

"No, you aren't going anywhere near him. I believe he really does mean to kill you." The chief of the boat had no glint of humor in his eye.

"You can't be serious!" I denied his worrying. "Chief, we are all on the same boat! I just saved his life! He won't kill me!"

But the Chief was serious, and he stuck to his guns. "You don't serve on the same boat, not anymore. He could sneak up from behind and hit you with a wrench, you wouldn't even see it coming. Sorry Pete. I am transferring you."

And that's how I got my first transfer, from screwing another sailor's ex-wife.

True story.

You can't make this shit up!

It ended up being for the best, the transfer. It's how I got to spend time down in Saint Thomas with the Underwater Demolition Team.

The water in Saint Thomas was nothing like the northern waters I had just come from. In the Caribbean, the water is warm, extra salty, and the color of turquoise.

I've mentioned that in those days the Navy Seals were called U.D.T. or Frogmen. They liked me because I could always get them good food. The meals they got served weren't real good, so I used my position as a cook to get them whatever they wanted.

I trained with them because they were tough and I like a challenge. When I tell you these are the toughest men on the planet I'm telling the truth. I have firsthand experience.

We would run, dive, and spar. We would practice fighting under water especially. Which of course I had just been reminded was extremely important in my line of work as the ships diver.

Saint Thomas was where I eventually began to train younger sailors how to withstand interrogations. It was because of this training program that the government awarded me the highest clearance. I was top secret, not even Barbara ever knew I had a "Q" clearance. I used to tease her with the knowledge I had access to.

One time while on a short leave, I told her to watch the papers. I said, "In two weeks, the leader of such and such country is going to 'commit suicide'."

When the papers confirmed my information two weeks later she was shocked.

"But how did you know it would happen, Pete?"

I loved to tease her so I would just laugh and tell her it was top secret. Which, of course, it was.

No, I never told my wife about the torture training or the "Harley girl" that got me kicked off my first sub. I knew better than to tell tales out of school. It's an ability I find many people lacking nowadays.

1995
Pete:

"Lucky for me you're still in town." Today is our last day in Dublin. Tomorrow we fly home for a week to take care of some business and to attend the big charity event for the shelter.

"No problem, Peter. You want to discuss a tech stock?" Karen Jones the CEO of my company, Money Trust, sits across the desk from me.

She's got an amazing resume for sure and years of experience on Wall Street. It was the late 1970s when she first handled some stock transactions for me, and she did so efficiently and competently.

Since then she's made me a ton of money. It was a no brainer putting her in charge of this aspect of my business. She's very good at her job, and I only prompt her occasionally when a startup catches my eye, or I read about a business of interest to me-- something I want to support and see succeed.

"What do you know about Apple Computer Company?"

"I know a little," she starts. "They've got a relatively new CEO." She pauses to think. "Spindler's the name, I think. They have a new product out-- Everyone is talking about their *Power Processor*. The company is doing better than it was, but they are not out of the trenches yet."

She knew a little. Hah! It makes me happy to know this woman is in charge of my investments. Her little is a whole lot!

Maybe I just trust women more with my money. That makes sense. Before she died, Barb had started investing in the stock market. It was her gig from the start, since I had no interest in it.

One day she let me know there was a company she'd like to invest in, and I told her to go ahead. Little did I realize we would make decent money off it!

I still own some of the stock Barb acquired, and every quarter a check arrives. The money from her stocks is donated to the Women's Shelter, but it's still making money nonetheless.

She was business savvy without any schooling on it, because she had common sense and she did her due diligence. She always kept up with world events and politics, and read at least four newspapers every day.

The stock market is a whole different ball game than real estate. We were well matched. I had my strengths and Barb had her own. I always went to her when I had a dilemma.

The first time I went to her with a problem we were still teenagers. I was on leave from the Navy and we were having a nice date. This was before we were married.

Since I was a cook in the Navy I knew my way around a kitchen and I had made her dinner, roasted chicken with corn on the cob and potatoes. She had surprised me in return with an apple pie. She was an amazing baker-- that apple pie was the best I'd ever tasted.

Of all the tasty things she cooked me while we were together, most of all I miss her apple pie. After all these years missing her I still think about that apple pie, and compare all others to it. None come even close to hers. It was the best feeling in the world to come home after months at sea and smell those warm apples when I walked in the door.

While I was on leave this particular time I of course had been checking up on my business. I had a foreman to continue building houses while I was at sea. When I came home I would make sure everything was on schedule and spend some time at the building sites working on whatever projects needed completing. Of course, I would also spend a bit of time looking for new land to build on.

Now I had plenty of money in the bank, and Mr. Burt still backed a huge portion of my houses, but that didn't change the fact that while a house was being built there was no money coming in, just out, in droves. I was writing check after check to the carpenters and electricians, but had to wait for a house to be finished and then sold in order to make my pay check.

I described this cash flow issue to a young Barb, as I said we weren't married yet, but I liked to discuss my business with her.

She thought about my dilemma for a minute or two and then declared her logical solution: "Why don't you use some of this money you're making to start building commercial buildings? Then you could charge rent and always make a monthly check, even if you aren't selling or building anything." It was a genius idea. So, I did it.

This step in commercial real estate was what started making me real money. I went from being a young businessman making a good deal more than the average joe to just plan rich in a very short time.

It was this money that gave me the opportunity to begin investing in companies and overseas. The old saying that you've got to have money to make money is most certainly true and Barbara was at the very center of my early success.

"Why the sudden interest in tech, may I ask?" Karen effectively brings my attention back to the present.

"You're always after me about diversifying," I evade.

"Yup, I do advise that, and occasionally I take the chance anyway and invest in a startup. Technology is growing exponentially whether we are talking computer or cell phones or the internet. But you are old school. You like stocking up in banks and old money." She waves her hand in my general direction, but I can tell she's joking around now. Always our conversations boil down to how old I'm getting and shouldn't I retire soon.

I wasn't dead yet! I could still get a girl in her twenties. "Actually, Elaine has been following the market, and she likes this company's product."

Karen's perfectly waxed eyebrow makes for the ceiling and she smirks, casting a long appreciative look out the door of my office where Elaine is standing at her desk talking on the phone. She's playing with the phone cord and absentmindedly sliding her leather pump on and off her foot.

"Elaine, huh?" Karen keeps her voice down because the doors are open. "Could have seen that one coming." She swings her chair back around to obscure the view of Elaine's fitted black dress.

"I don't know what you are insinuating, honey. All I said was Elaine gave me the idea."

"Uh-huh, over breakfast."

I smile and neaten a stack of papers, but remain silent.

"It's too bad." Karen glances over at Elaine once more, "I was going to ask her to dinner myself."

Elaine has found her seat now, and looks up to notice us staring. Totally unselfconscious, the beauty flashes up her biggest Cheshire cat grin.

"I'm sure Charlotte, would have something to say about that" I joke with Karen, bringing up her longtime girlfriend.

Karen raises her brow again. "Ah, Char and I are on a little break."

I don't know what to say, they've been together for years, at least a decade. "Sorry to hear that."

Karen looks angry. Whether it's for discussing personal matters or because she's pissed at her partner I can't fathom. "I'm sure you'll work it out." I add.

Karen waves her hand dismissively, "If she wants to paint pictures of mountains in New Hampshire then let her."

I decide to joke around and lighten the mood. "Then again, now that I think about it, maybe Elaine does swing that way?" Actually, it could be true. I muse, she is young and free, she could like both men and woman.

People these days have more sexual freedom than ever before. People now are openly gay, bi, transgender, heck-- married couples swing and talk about it over dinner these days. It really is an amazing world!

I think my wife would have liked the way things had changed socially. I remember how she used to notice women. She would comment on the beauty of a women on the street or the cut of her dress. To my knowledge, she had never acted on this admiration for the female form, but it was nice in a way. We used to admire other woman together. I wonder now what my lovely wife would have been like had she grown up in a time like this.

Elaine catches my eye.

I must be a lucky bastard. Here I am sitting in my office with the CEO of one my many companies. Then, there's Elaine. I know she is making sure everything's running smoothly out there, all over the world.

I don't know what all the fuss is about over women in the workplace, and gender equality. Sure, women make great moms, but who says they can't make great company heads as well?

Barb would have made a great CEO. Heck, she pretty much was. She basically ran my business for the two years I was at sea. She had all the right qualities to be in charge: brilliantly smart, tough, and darn stubborn when it came down to it. Which can be a plus when people know they can't push you around.

Karen and Elaine are the same as Barb. They know when to be tough and they know when to be soft. Elaine calls it her 'sugar' and her 'spice'. And I've personally seen Karen dominate in an industry grossly overpopulated by men. It's obvious to me that gender doesn't have anything to do with being competent in business, and my wife showed me from the start. She was the boss.

"Somebody's got to be the boss."

1995
Elaine:

We flew in last night. It's weird to be back stateside. I guess I'll have to stop by and see my mom while I'm over here. Luckily, we are here only for a week. Once the annual fundraiser is over we will be back in the air and on our way to the Caribbean to check in on PB Holdings.

We're staying central; the capital city is a good place to set up shop for our short stay. The hotels are nice, the restaurants decent and the trip to Peter's home town from here is minimal. Just a forty minute drive northeast.

It's just after sunrise. We're at the gym getting a quick workout before starting the day. Basically, I'm a spectator, since I know next to nothing about boxing. Merely listening to one person hit another makes me queasy. My session with one of the trainers is nearly over and we're finishing up with jump ropes.

Jumping rope as an adult always puts me in mind of childhood games. Hours spent in the summer sun with all the neighborhood kids playing double Dutch, or seeing who could jump the longest without tripping. I can't help but smile as I hit the one hundred mark and start my count back down. One to ninety, then one to eighty, then one to seventy, all the way back down, one to ten. One thousand double-under jumps. That would probably have made me neighborhood champion that summer.

My trainer for the day is named Kyle. "Why are you smiling?" He looks pleasantly surprised. "I've never really seen anyone smile during this particular workout before."

I feel winded as I laugh aloud and tell him, "I guess I just love to jump rope!" Just to prove it I do a side swing on each side before continuing my double-unders. He shakes his head but smiles good naturedly. He's kind of cute. In a young sort of way. Not really my type, but he's fit. I bet he would be pretty decent in bed. Gosh, it is easy to let thoughts wander. I smile back at him and he blushes a little.

Oh good, I've got his mind wandering now too. This makes me feel bold and alive. What a wonderful feeling, I revel in the feeling as the blood moves hot through my veins and my heart pounds. The jump rope wizzes in a steady rhythm.

Pete is in the ring. Unlike me, boxing isn't new to him. He looks strong and focused. Jab, jab, with his elbow high to protect his face. A left hook, an upper cut, all precise and fluid, calculated movements. I can almost hear his mind working. 'Gloves up, move faster, step lighter.'

But I know from experience that the guy in the ring shouldn't be impressed with the precision of these movements. What he really should be on the lookout for was Pete's right cross.

A few months back we attended a real estate conference. Pete was just tagging along since he knew it all already, but I had so much to learn. Honestly, it's probably just easier sometimes for him to send me to someone else to be trained, and I know he has fond memories of his early real estate career. Traveling all over the country, attending seminars, sometimes speaking at them. And, of course, seducing as many women as possible along the way.

This particular conference was on using lease options to buy and sell properties. The day had been spent taking notes, and I was a little stir crazy. Pete was up in his room working, so when I was invited by some other conference goers to the hotel bar for a drink I was all too happy to comply.

It was a nice bar, all dark wood and glass shelves. Everyone was dressed to impress, including me in a tight purple number. The night had started off fun, a huge group of the younger salespeople grabbing a drink and talking about our fledgling carriers-- how many properties we each owned, or how many current listings. Some complained about dealing with tenants.

'How crazy this is,' I thought to myself. 'Here I am holding my own, in a room full of professionals!'

As the crowd started to thin out I realized I had surpassed my normal martini limit. How many had I had? Three? Four? These guys just kept buying me drinks. Maybe I should have stuck with wine or beer.

The shame I felt that night comes back to me as I remember. How could I have been so naïve? Watching Pete fight brings the evening back into sharp focus.

As I was trying to leave, one of my drunken male companions followed me out. He followed me up to my floor. Creeper!

All I really remember is holding onto my room key and saying, "No, really. No. I'm going to bed." Then Pete was there. Wham! The right cross, and a wild look in his eyes.

Talk about sobering up quick! The air seemed to clear just a little.

"Oh my god!" I remember whispering it because I didn't want Pete to get into trouble, and there was this dude in an over-large cheap suit laying crumpled on the junction between beige hallway wall and tacky hunter green carpet. Without hesitation, Peter picked up the guy, whose name I can't even remember, and deposited him in one of the elevators.

Meanwhile I'm repeating my whispered mantra of, "Oh my god. Oh my god."

Pete just walks back to me and puts a protective arm around my shoulder. "Don't worry, he won't remember a thing."

Which was true, I guess. We flew back to Dublin the next morning. I haven't touched anything more than a sip of champagne since. The obligatory sip during a toast or event, that's it. I never want to be in a situation like that again.

My cell phone rings, bringing me back to the moment, the gym and its dirty socks smell.

"Can't catch a break huh?" Kyle try's a joke.

"No rest for the weary!" I chuck the jump rope onto my gym bag and dig around for the bleeping Nokia. First a swig from my water bottle, now pull the phone antennae out with my teeth. "Hello, Elaine here." I try to catch my breath.

It's Harold Clay, our real estate guru and my most frequent contact, since commercial and rental properties were fast becoming my area of expertise.

"Elaine, I tried Peter's phone, but he's not picking up."

"That's right, Clay, he's in the ring."

"Ask him to take a break. This is about Beijing. Another group is going after it. We have to move fast."

"Gotcha." I move the phone away from my face, stick two fingers in my mouth and give a great loud whistle. Just like my dad used to do.

Pete knows the sound, and holds up both hands as he backs away from his opponent. The guy bounces around acting tough. He looks tough, all muscle and sweat. Pete looks to me expectantly.

"It's Clay. Atlas Firm is going after our high-rise in Beijing."

"Son of a bitch." He's out of the ring and has my phone out of earshot in seconds.

The gym guys all stare at me. All I can do is smile and shrug. "Work." I mumble and start to gather my gear back up.

1995
Pete:

I'm sweating and breathing heavy. I wipe down with a towel and take an extra swig of cool water. A few more seconds to compose myself should suffice before bringing the phone to my ear.

With a deep meditative breath, my heart slows a fraction and I'm ready to discuss the business at hand: acquiring a new high rise, my first in China.

"Harold. Good morning."

"Hello, Mr. Pete. Sorry to call so early, I wanted to check in before moving forward."

"If it's really Atlas Group, calm down. They don't have a leg to stand on. We just have to move up the time table."

"Right. Got it. Just wanted you to be aware I'm moving forward. First thing in the morning."

There was a twelve-hour time difference. It was the end of Harold's day, yet ours was just beginning. He sounded confident, not too worried, just tired. His team was efficient, but they'd probably been working like crazy the last few days.

"Great, I'll have Elaine follow up with you afterwards. And when all's said and done, take your crew out for a night on the town. Beijing is supposed to be a fun place."

He laughs. "When all's said and done, I'm going to sleep. Damn jet lag!"

I reprimand him good naturedly, "Don't forget to celebrate the wins, my friend."

"I won't, Pete." He switches to my first name casually. I guess that's to be expected after so many years working together.

I put Harold Clay in charge of my brokerage nearly fifteen years ago, now. He was a tough guy who grew up in a tough neighborhood in Harlem, NY. Initially that's why he got the job. Harold was a young kid then, but even so he wasn't a man you would think about pushing around. I had learned over the years that this was a good quality to have as a landlord.

As I got to know him I realized the kid had a good head on his shoulders as well, so instead of just using him as muscle I started to mentor him in real estate.

He'd come a long way since then. He wasn't just a landlord for me anymore-- we had high rises all over the world now. His job these days was to make sure all the other guys were just as tough and just as good about making sure we got our money.

That's what it all comes down to in business: not being polite, not running a great meeting or worrying about the daily ins and outs. Just plain and simple, get the money.

We had buildings in all the major cities: Manhattan, Chicago, San Francisco, Dublin, London, Moscow. Harold was the public face of my real estate company. To the public eye, he was at the top. But he worked for me, and just like Brewster Newy, he was in place to keep me out of the limelight.

In the beginning, the high rises were for Barbara. She had always dreamed we'd own one someday. I'll never forget the first time she went to New York with me and looked at those tall buildings looming up all around us. She looked like the worst sort of tourist, and I thought it was adorable. We were both country bumpkins through and through, but that was alright, because I knew someday we'd own those buildings.

It was December of 1959 and I had just been discharged from the Navy. We were in the yards down in Philly. Already my wife, Barbara came down and met me. Her mom had little Pete. After one night in Philadelphia I drove us up to New York.

I splurged and got us a room at the Hotel Astor in Times Square. It wasn't a very tall building but from its rooftop garden the view was amazing. There was always a party up there and oftentimes a famous musician playing on the bandstand.

We stood up there and she was so impressed by it all. She asked me then if ever we could buy one of those grand buildings. I assured her that it wouldn't be too many more years and we would have even more than one.

The Hotel Astor was torn down in the sixties. A high-rise office tower stands in its place, the mark of progress.

1995

Elaine:

Pete doesn't look worried when he comes back into the room. "Can you make sure to follow up with Mr. Clay around..." He thinks for a moment. "Eleven PM tonight?"

"Sure thing, boss man." I'm joking, but I can tell from his face he doesn't like that nickname. Oh well, nothing a smile can't fix.

Shaking his head like he can't figure something out, he climbs back into the ring. I am beginning to wonder how much longer we will spend in this gym when I realize Pete is no longer defending. Something has shifted in his attitude in the last few minutes.

He's been a fighter since youth-- always the tough guy, as he tells me. But it was in the Navy that he learned to box. It was during his years at sea after he befriended the Naval Heavyweight Champion.

I guess that's a big deal, being the Navy's Champion. I could tell you the story by heart now, that's how often I've heard it. Pete does love to reminisce.

John was bigger than Pete and well trained in the precise sport of boxing, and one day he asks this new cook to spar with him. At the time a submarine tour could be as long as three months.

After the subs switched from diesel to nukes they could go six months, but this was before that, and three months is still a long time to be under water. While living on the sub there's no room to train, so John had to try to keep in shape while on the base and during shore leave.

I think Peter had to have been about eighteen at the time.

Never having boxed before, he managed to block the first jabs, but Pete was not expecting that first real punch. It split his lip open, and it hurt. He tells me, "So I hit him back!" *Bam!* A wild and angry right handed punch with all his weight behind it.

His new buddy John went into defensive mode, and here came the uppercuts. Peter describes seeing red. "I was so pissed I picked that son of a bitch up off the ground and I threw him out of the ring!"

Sometimes he mimics throwing the guy, arms tense, muscles remembering the adrenaline of lifting a grown man and flinging him over the ropes.

"I jumped out there and went after him ready to kill him."

And John jumps up and yells, "Woah, Petey! Woah. What the heck did you throw me out of the ring for?"

"What the heck did you hit me so hard for?" Still furious but calming at this point, the red starts to fade, vision clearing.

"Well..." John may have been a little embarrassed to admit, "You hurt me!"

At this point in the telling Peter usually dissolves into a fit of laughter, remembering how they almost killed each other. I imagine they were fast friends.

I can see it all in clarity now, as I watch the same man fight a much younger opponent. The mania just below the surface, the fighter's blazing spirit burning for a win. Who knows if it's the actual fight, the deal in China, or the long day ahead. He steps forward, jab, jab, cross, landing that wild right punch.

Winner.

1959
Pete:

He showed me the picture: a cute girl with a wide smile and childlike dimples. He asked me, as was typical of sailors, or any man in the service at the time, "Have you got a sweetheart waiting for you?" There was a lot of downtime while traveling on the sub. I read a lot of books in those days. We were on our way down to Saint Thomas.

I thought about all of my lovers, but Barb popped into my head and made me smile. I told him, "Well, I've got a couple. But only one picture."

I went to my bunk to fish it out. The bunks on those old boats were stacked three high. I had made sure to get a top bunk, not a middle or lower one. The guys liked to wait until they had to fart and then run over to stick their asses right into those lower bunks and let it loose. There was nowhere to go! Often times the sailor in his bunk would smash his head trying to scramble out to avoid the smell.

The picture was from my last leave in June. It was of me and Barb. I had taken her to a dance at the high school. She was graduating at sixteen. We screwed like rabbits that night in celebration.

The picture's black and white, though I know her dress had been pale blue lace, a dancing dress with a full skirt. It matched her eyes perfectly.

I was in uniform, as it was cheaper than getting a tux.

Barb's photo got the necessary praise. And how could it not, she was gorgeous in every way, from her swimmer's body to her full lips and thick wavy hair.

The call sounded and we all jumped. We were surfacing, riding the rest of the way to the Caribbean base on the surface. Time for some fresh air and smoking out under the open sky. Mostly everyone on board smoked. I didn't do it much, because I could tell the difference in my lungs right away, and that wasn't good for diving. Smoking is a nasty, choking habit, that usually made the whole boat a smoky haze while we were submerged. After we surfaced all the guys would be up top smoking so the air would be clear below. I went up to stand in the sunshine and watch the land approach over the ocean waves.

The sun was blaring, but the cool ocean breeze saved us from overheating. It felt good to be topside. That's about when I heard the short directional blasts of a ship's horn. We were arriving alongside another batch of sailors. Not submarine sailors, though. We catcalled over to the guys on the deck of the cruiser. There's a sort of rivalry that's always existed between us, submariners and the other sailors. The long and short of it is we felt the boys on the top side boats were spoiled and soft. On a sub we lived cramped and didn't see the daylight or get fresh air for long stretches of time.

Whatever, we were on the same side, I guess, but that didn't stop the rivalry. All I know is this would be the second time I would come close to killing my friend John.

All for a bet. A really big bet, on a fight I set up and told absolutely everyone about.

"I never worried about marrying her. I loved her."

1959
Pete:

"... "John says to me, "I'm gonna kill you, Pete." My arm was draped casually over Barb's shoulders while we walked together along the sidewalk. We had just left Raymond's after having shared some ice-cream.

I continue with my story of the big fight, "'All right, John, okay, you do that.' And I helped him into his rack. He was like a dead weight barely holding himself upright. He coughed, spit up some blood... that's not good, spitting up blood, you see. Then he groans.

'I mean it. When I get out of this bed, I'm gonna kill you.' I let him go and he collapsed. He was so sore and tired."

Here's how it happened: those cruiser boys were all at the local bar the first night we were back to base. After a few rounds they start telling us that they have the best boxer in the whole Navy on their very own ship, might even be the best boxer ever. Well, I couldn't sit and listen to that, so I said, "We've got the Naval Heavyweight Champ living on our boat, so you either don't know what the fuck you're talking about or you're lying."

"Oh, yeah! Well, I smell a fight!"

You're damn straight we set up a fight, along with near a hundred bets placed on both sides. I was the bookie, and set up the time and place of the fight. My friend John wasn't too happy.

"I can't fight tomorrow!"

"Why not? It's already set up!" He had to fight. I'd be in deep shit if he didn't.

"Pete, I've been at sea for months!"

"That doesn't matter, so has your opponent."

"But I live on a sub, I can't train on a sub!"

"You'll be fine, I'm sure they were just blowing smoke."

They weren't. Their guy was good. The fight went three full rounds. If you don't know about boxing, let me tell you, that's a really long fight. And they were pretty evenly matched. If John were in peak shape it would have been an easy win. Unfortunately, he wasn't, so it took him three full rounds to win. But win he did. Our John was most certainly the Naval Champion.

I think he was pretty serious about killing me. That is until the captain of our boat came in and told Johnny he appreciated the win, considering how much money he had bet on the fight.

"You've got a full weeks' basket leave coming to you, son. Nicely done."

Basket leave is paid in full leave, and it's a rare treat! John forgot about killing me after that. But I think it was a close call, for both of us... ..."

I stopped telling my story to see what was up. "Barb?" She didn't seem like she was paying attention. But I thought this was a pretty good story.

"Yeah?" I remember her looking a little frail, which was way out of character.

"You've been sort of quiet all night. Everything okay?" When I told the guys at the building site the fight story they had laughed like crazy. Maybe it was guy thing?

"Oh no, it really is good laugh. It's just, I have something I need to tell you." I'd never seen her so nervous before. Usually she was confident and calm. I was just parking the car at our favorite spot and turned to give her my full attention.

She just blurted it out, "Well, you see, I've missed my period."

It's like a ton of bricks hitting you in the chest. I knew what it meant, but it took a few moments for my mouth to catch up with my brain.

It's a testament to this young girl's strength that she just sat in silence waiting. That she had been so patient all this time. Three months. I had been gone three months! And I knew it was mine. There was no question. I knew what kind of girl she was. She had been with only me.

I should have known better; I did know better. We both did!

When you have sex as often as we had been a baby was almost a sure thing.

There was nothing to say. I hugged her close and she cried. And she kept on crying. Four days later she was crying when we stood up there in front of the priest. I kept thinking to myself, 'What the hell am I doing here?'

But I knew what the hell I was doing. She was pregnant at seventeen and it was 1958. When you got a girl pregnant back then, you married her. If I hadn't she would have been ruined. I couldn't do that to her, not to Barbara. And so, she became my wife, the one and only.

Neither of us wanted to get married. We were so young! I'll never forget our wedding night. It was a Tuesday evening, in September of 1958. We went to the Episcopal church in our hometown. Me in my uniform, and she in that pale blue lace dress that matched her eyes so perfectly. It was the last week of summer but that evening was cool, the leaves just starting to turn red and gold at the edges.

I remember Barb shivering just once, so I put my arm around her while I walked her to the truck. I wonder now if it was nerves or just the breeze that caused her to tremor. She leaned into me and we warmed one another. Apple blossoms, she smelled like apple blossoms that night. My Barb loved flowers.

To the casual passerby, we could have been going to a dance, just like we had done three months beforehand wearing the same spiffy outfits.

She cried and cried through the whole ceremony. It was awful. I don't know what the priest was thinking. I knew what I was thinking-- 'Get me the hell out of here!'

We both had to be up at the crack of dawn. There's still work to do even if you aren't out to sea, you still have to report for work at the base. My new wife was off to work at the nearby university.

She had graduated high school at sixteen with honors. All her hard work had landed her a good position in the university president's office. She toyed with the idea of going to college, but never did. I guess we both just got too busy, and then there was the baby.

It never ceases to amaze me how much Barb accomplished while I was away at sea. She kept the books alright, and made sure everything with the early company stayed on track. There was no hesitation in her. If she needed to go to one of the job sites to handle a problem with a crew member or a lumber shortage, whatever the issue, she would take care of it. And she took care of our little one while maintaining her job at the university. She found time for it all and never complained.

It still amazes me.

I had quickly arranged for us to rent a small apartment just off base. We couldn't live with the other sailors!

The apartment was located in a little white house that had been turned into a two family. We only had access to the front room, but it was by the sea so I thought Barb would like it. She did love the sea so much.

That first night she got to the house and kept crying on and off.

"I just want to go home," she kept saying.

I tried my best to make her like our new place. I made love to her gently and soothed her as best I could.

Finally, she fell asleep in my arms and I held her close so she wouldn't feel alone or scared. We were so young. Teenagers still, the both of us.

I held onto her that night hoping she would settle and be happy in our new life together. I was pleasantly surprised to see how well she got on after that. I loved watching her at the building sites, speaking her mind to the contractors, and having them jump to.

It wasn't long before my wife captivated every corner of my heart with her brilliance. But it was on that first night as husband and wife as she slept in my arms, that I vowed to work harder than ever before. I would do anything to make her happy. She's the only women I ever loved.

"It is my favorite activity, second to nothing, even making money."

1995
Elaine:

The house looks good. It's freshly painted, the siding looks spotless. The yard seems a little blank now, since we took up all the over grown shrubs. It's ok, I'm not worried-- the new owners can plant something. I'll just put some grass seed down and make it look clean. A blank slate. That's what people want now a days.

Actually, looking at the house now, I began to think I shouldn't sell it.

There's a spirit to this place that not all houses have. It's more than a box with a roof and windows. The entry way juts out a little and is built of brick. This brick wall slopes down gracefully all the way to the corner of the home and the two small living room windows are set within it. I know very well that above that door where a round window hangs, the interior upstairs hall houses a charming little window seat. It's set at the most perfect vantage point to place a cozy reader level with the canopy of the trees outside.

Yes, it is a charming little place. Maybe I'll hold on to the property and just rent it out while I'm still stationed in Europe most of the year.

That is after all, how Pete made his bucks back in the day, renting out houses, apartments, and offices. The list goes on, but I'm not there yet.

I'm just getting started. This is my first solo project. I'm hoping to use what I've learned from Pete to set myself up with a strong safety net. Also, it would be nice to show him I've been listening.

All his stories are more than just tall tales, they are a textbook of information about how this guy started at sixteen and built his fortune. At twenty-five, I have some serious catching up to do; by this point in his life Peter was already a millionaire, and owned a high-rise building.

"Bye, Mark!" I yell as I climb up into Pete's 1985 Dodge pickup truck. "I'll pop by tomorrow morning!" Mark's the handyman I hired to work on the property. He can do all sorts of things, and knows all the local electricians and carpenters. He has done pretty well over the last couple of weeks while I've been away. My house is almost done.

"Alright, see you tomorrow, then! Bright and early!" He flashes a big smile in my direction, and then continues his task of cleaning up the worksite for the evening.

I slam the door to the truck and start the engine. I love this truck. It's old but well cared for and has a huge bed on it to haul equipment around in.

I've got tile grout and paint all over my jeans. Finishing tile in the bathroom and painting all the interior walls will do that to a good pair of jeans, though I think I like them better now. Tomorrow is trim day and then we will do the final clean up. I also decide suddenly to put some flowering bushes on either side of the front door. Maybe hydrangea?

This project has come along pretty quick, though it probably seemed even quicker to me since I split my time between here, Dublin, and St. Eustatius.

It has taken some getting used to, balancing all these plates, but I like a challenge, and the everyday rush has quickly become my norm.

It was just a couple months ago when we spent a few days in London that I finally made the decision to buy this investment property. I felt it was time to test out all of Pete's lessons.

We were in London on business. Peter had a board meeting at one of his banks. He had sizeable investments in many large banks, and when you owned enough of a bank, you often became a board member and have the ability to pull the strings of upper management.

In the beginning of his career Pete made it a goal to establish relationships with these banks, and then used their money to begin acquiring much bigger investment properties; namely high-rise complexes in the major cities around the world. Luckily Barb did live to see the day they purchased their first high-rise. Of course, it was in New York City.

"She loved to look up at those buildings," Pete tells me. "She always wanted to own one."

Now he has a ton of them.

"It was easy after I was rich," he told me that day while we were walking around London, thinking about where to have dinner.

"You see, Elaine, if you want to borrow ten grand and you go to apply for a loan they want your first born. But if you are rich already, you can ask for ten million bucks and they'll hand it over without blinking."

I laughed but he was serious.

"I'm telling you the truth. One time when I was twenty-three years old, I got a one and a half million dollar commitment over lunch for a building I wanted to put up! There was no paperwork! No credit checks!"

"Well, I'm not in your situation." I spoke up. "I still need to sign away my first born."

"Elaine, I told you I'll lend you the money," he said.

"Pete, I want to do this on my own. I don't need a hand out."

"It's not a hand out!" He smirked. "But don't worry. I'll give you a good deal!"

I couldn't help but laugh at his carefree nature. Always with the jokes. "I wouldn't touch one of your mortgages with a hundred-foot pole!"

Pete pretended to look hurt. "Elaine, I help people get into homes." He put his hand on his chest in a mock display of a chivalry.

He had alright, a ton of people, and he laughed all the way to the bank, literally. If someone was coming to him for a loan, they usually couldn't get it elsewhere, so he would give it to them but at a decent rate of interest.

"Yeah, I know, back in the day. At 7%, 'no appraisals, no inspection, no upfront costs.'" I said the last part in a deep voice while gesturing my hand as much like Pete as I could manage.

"Are you mocking me, honey?" He stopped in the middle of the sidewalk with his hand on my arm.

I swept his hair off his forehead and smiled getting closer to him. "You bet I am."

He kissed me, and I let him. I always let him.

"Let's go back to the hotel," he said after a moment. "Now."

"But you promised me dinner!" I pretended to be upset, but I wanted to go back the hotel as well. It had been a long day staring at him across a conference table.

He responded by practically picking me up and starting off down the sidewalk again, this time in the direction of the hotel, "I'll order room service."

My sigh was fake. "Room service again." But then I made him stand still and kissed him to let him know I was just as keen to make it back to the hotel as he was. He leaned into me returning the kiss. "Let's get a taxi," I breathed.

That night I sat up making plans. I wanted to flip a house, and I would do so on my own merit. Pete couldn't help but look proud when I told him I'd do it without his help.

"If you can buy the property yourself, you are better off," he told me. Meaning if I could manage, I should purchase without a mortgage. I did have savings, just enough to buy a piece of crap house that needed lots of love to make it habitable again.

So I did it, took a chunk out of my saving and bought a small house at auction. I used the value of the land to take out a line of home equity. I felt this was better than a mortgage because the interest rate on equity is usually half what a conventional mortgage is. And since the loan was for construction I only have to pay the interest for the first six months. This was the money I used for renovation and to pay Mark. If I keep the house and rent it out, the rental income on it will more than cover the small equity loan and the taxes. I could always sell it in the future if I wanted, and then the property values would almost certainly be higher.

It hadn't been in horrible shape, actually. The foundation was sound and the copper pipes were all in place, needing only a little soldering to stop some minor leaks.

I put in new electrical, but most houses this old need updating in that department. The hardwood floors were a plus, but man what a pain it had been to sand those suckers down! I did as much of the work as I could alongside Mark, and I'll admit to being very proud of how beautifully they turned out.

Pete tells me that in the early 1980s there were a lot of houses on the market, and it was tough times so people weren't buying. He decided to buy a bunch up real cheap and rent them out.

"People always need a place to live," he likes to say. "Even if they can't buy a house, they still need a place to live!"

Around a couple years ago, Pete and Harold decided to sell off a bunch of them. "I laughed all the way to the bank," Pete says.

That's what I'd like to do. If the market falls again, I'd like to be in a place to snatch up some deals. Then I can hold on to them. It's call 'buy and hold'. It's a good bit of advice. The rent money from the houses is just cash in your pocket.

I turn the truck onto Pete's road. His property is on a huge one hundred acre plot of land. As I cross the small river that runs alongside the property I can't help but think how idyllic this country setting is. It must have been a wonderful feeling as a young family to move here.

Halfway up the drive I see smoke coming from a big metal barrel and piles of empty boxes on the pavement. Pete's been burning something.

Inside I holler, "Hey, Pete, I'm here, you almost ready to go? I'm gonna hop in the shower. I'll be ready in ten!"

He doesn't respond, but I know he's here. I can hear the radio in the other room. Shrugging, I strip down and pull my hair up high on my head. I don't have time to wash and dry it; we have to go and taste the food samples for the fundraiser.

1995
Peter:

I see Elaine pull up the drive in my old pickup truck. I love that truck; it's got bench seats which makes it really easy for someone to slide right up next to you. It also allows enough room for other activities. I'm game for a lot of stuff, but sex in bucket seats is never comfortable.

Elaine's been out working on her house all day. She looks good, even in ripped jeans all covered in paint. Especially in ripped jeans, actually.

It's nice to see her trying projects like this. Her excitement reminds me of myself all those years ago, when I first had the idea to start building houses.

When Elaine first started working for me she was still a little unsure about what she was capable of. I put her on a few local projects like managing the commercial buildings here in town, making sure the renovations for new businesses were going smoothly, or running the annual fundraiser for the Women's Shelter. This is, I can tell, one of her favorite projects. This year she has impressed me with a bigger, more spectacular event. I have a feeling she will manage to bring in more money than ever.

This means we can give out more scholarships to some of the kids and young women who've needed to stay in the shelter.

Just recently I had the pleasure of attending the graduation of one of our past residents. She's in her thirties, a mom of three, and she graduated with honors from the nearby university. The very same university my late wife used to work in.

It had been a good day. I took her and her family out to eat afterwards. The kids ordered grilled cheeses and talked about how they would go to college one day. They all seemed so happy.

Barbara would have been overjoyed to see what was becoming of the little shelter we started all those years ago.

"Hey." Elaine's head appears in the office doorway, bringing me back to the present. "What's with all the boxes outside?"

"Oh," I respond, "just burning a bunch of old files. Don't need them anymore." I check my watch we need to head out soon.

Elaine is pulling on socks and has donned a clean pair of jeans and a white tee shirt. An all-American girl, with her wavy hair piled up on top of her head. She looks amazing and smells like soap. "Cool." She says, "I Guess you finally got up into the attic then."

I'd been talking about cleaning stuff out for a while. She takes her long hair down and shakes it out, coming into the room. "Whatcha got there?"

I indicate the stained papers and envelopes on the desk in front of me. "These are the letters I wrote to Barbara while I was in the Navy."

"Really?" She stays back just enough to show she doesn't want to intrude on my privacy, but I can tell she's excited. Elaine loves to hear my stories. Deep down I think she might be some kind of romantic. Oh well, I can't fix everything.

"Yup." I run my fingers through my hair. "I was honestly just trying to figure out if I should get rid of them."

"Get rid of them?" Her face is appalled. Yup, she's a romantic alright. "You can't get rid of them!"

"Sure I can." I point at my temple. "It's all up here anyway."

"I know, but they are a part of history. Your history. Don't you want someday for people to know who Peter, the Bad Ass Biker, Naval Hero, Self-Made Billionaire and Humanitarian, really was?"

"No, I don't." Privacy is crucial to me. One of the reasons I still blend in so well here in my home town, is because people don't really know even a fraction of the stuff I've done.

They know I've got money, but they don't know how much. For all they know I'm just Pete, an old townie, who had done pretty well in real estate and who likes to spend his money on fast cars and traveling.

Elaine sighs at me and looks annoyed, which is just adorable.

"I wish I had a camera in my head so I could take a picture of you right now." She smiles at my old joke. I say it all the time, but I always mean it.

The way the light hit her jaw just then, how it made her long wavy auburn hair glow. It would have been a stunning picture.

She switches back to the topic at hand. "Honestly, though, do you really want to burn these?"

I stand up and try not to sound too melodramatic. "It will be easier than burying her was." Drama is not something I do.

Elaine makes a sad sound, so I decide to tell her a happy story. A story for the romantic inside her.

"Have I ever told you about the time I took Barbara on our belated honeymoon?"

Elaine loves a good story she turns to me intrigued. "Not in complete detail, no."

"It was a couple weeks after our wedding. I was allowed some leave so we could celebrate our marriage. Barb was so excited. She'd never left the country before."

I walk Elaine into the kitchen and busy myself making coffee while I tell the story. It's a good story. Barb and I were happy to get away for a bit and just be young and in love. She really was my dearest friend, Barb was. I miss her so much.

I think that's what's up with me lately. I've been in my head so much. It must be because I miss my wife. I really do.

"She was the woman for me. I'll marry no one else, but I would marry her again and again in a heartbeat..."

October 1958

Saint Eustatius is an island located in the West Indies. At less than thirteen square miles, you might miss it on your way from Anguilla to Saint Kitts. This is where I chose to take Barb for our honeymoon. We stayed in a tiny beach house on a long-deserted stretch of beach. It was barely a hut, but we were in paradise, so what more could we need?

A couple of locals helped haul our suitcases in, and left discretely with a nice fat tip.

Barb went straight to the windows and doors and worked at pulling them all open.

"Why would you shut out this beautiful breeze?" She laughed in the salty air blowing up from the nearby waves. I could tell she liked it here very much; she looked so carefree and young. Then again, she was barely seventeen, and hidden under her carefully tucked blouse was the tiny little bump. The just-barely-visible indicator that soon we would be parents.

I remember my first task was unpacking the suitcases. On a sub, you have very little space so you have to be neat. It was habit for me to secure my bunk first.

When the shirts were all neatly placed in a drawer beside my slacks I heard Barbra exclaim.

"The ocean is right here! Look, my toes are in the sand one step out the door!"

I smiled over at her, slinging one of her dresses onto a hanger. "Look at all these palm trees-- you know I've only ever seen them in pictures before?"

"Yup, they're everywhere around here. And all full of coconuts. Don't let one hit your head! The locals say that's when you go 'coco-loco'!" I laughed at the joke.

My young bride was anxious for our honeymoon to be perfect, and I could tell she wanted me to pay attention to her, but I would never have guessed what she did next. She was bold in her own ways, but usually so shy and reserved. She really was a good girl; I'm not sure why she wanted to be with a dog like me.

But on this trip she was newly my wife and in a very secluded place.

"Pete, have you ever swam in the sea naked? I never have, though it sounds nice, doesn't it?"

"Huh?" I stopped in the middle of silk camisole organization.

Her back was to me and she smiled over her shoulder. Her dress was on the ground. What was left of her undergarments dangled from her fingers. With a flick of her wrist she threw them in my direction and boldly walked out onto the deserted beach toward the waves.

I dropped the silk, shocked. Mesmerized, I followed her, slowly at first then I picked up speed, shedding my own garments on the way to the sea. Having only discarded my top and shoes I waded in with my pants still on. What did

I care when there was a naked woman diving into the water ahead of me? She was so graceful in the water it was like dancing. It seemed to me that we fit so well together sexually because of our kindred training as swimmers. We both loved to be in water. I loved to imagine that spending all that time swimming had given us a certain grace and poise that other humans simply didn't possess.

When she came up for air, we clung to each other. There was no one to see us, but I don't think it would have mattered. At that moment Barbara was the only other person in the world.

I'll never forget that day when my proper Christian wife was made bold by the Caribbean sun and salty air. Oh, it was a wonderful honeymoon.

It was after these wonderful sexual encounters that Barbara and I would get most of our work done. At the beginning, it felt a lot like dreaming. We would lay in bed tangled together, and we would talk about our plans for the business. Barb would say she wanted high rises and I would explain the process we might follow to gain some. Or she would tell me about new companies or products on the market.

A few days into our trip to Statia—our name for it-- Barb turns to me and says, "Can we buy land here? Wouldn't it be nice to call a piece of this heavenly place ours?"

"Sure thing, honey." I kissed her on the nose.

She thought I was mocking her. "No, I'm serious, Pete! Do you think we could buy land here and build a little place? Just a little place where we could escape when we needed to."

"I'm serious, too, honey. You want to own this place, I'll get it."

"Really? Even if I wanted the whole island?" she joked.

"Done!"

"Oh, you are a fool!" She threw a pillow in my direction playfully. "And don't call me honey!"

It's a habit of mine to call girls honey. I've always done it and never thought much of it. But Barb had noticed and she would get upset and say, "Why do you call everyone honey?"

"Easy, that way I don't say the wrong name!" Oh, that got her good and mad. I did stop calling my wife honey, but it didn't stop me from using it on everyone else!

We purchased a chunk of land on Eustatius not long after that. It was a huge banana plantation on the side of the Quill.

The Quill is a dormant volcano. I used to run up the side of it in twenty minutes, surprising all the locals at how fast I was. It was a lovely place covered in trees, and inside the crater left by the volcano was the most luscious rain forest. We used to love to hike around in there and explore.

For a time when I was the largest non-native land holder on the entire island. But that was before I gave most of the land back to the local government so they could establish a national park on the Quill. At least now I know the land is protected, untouched, just the way we left it.

As a toddler, my son would run around on the beaches and climb the rain-drenched trees while Barbara laughed and taught him games.

My son was a good boy. Barbara had a way with him. They were a good team. She knew him well enough and paid the right amount of attention, and he was independent enough that he didn't need her every second. He never did fuss much, even as a baby, unless he was hungry. Then he could sure give a good scream.

It would have been wonderful to have more time with him. He was a neat kid.

"I like to have a million bucks cash laying around."

1995
Pete:

Lunch with the FBI is always a trip, especially when the agent just happens to be an old high school buddy of yours.

"Pete," says Lou, "what's this I hear about you and a lunch date with the leader of the Hell's Angels?"

I look at him over the top of my menu but don't say anything.

He gives up after a few moments of my silence and snorts out a short, amused laugh. "Look at you! You're the only guy I know who can have a meeting with the leader of an organization like that one week, then the next, you have lunch with me, the head of the state's FBI division. You are one tricky guy! One tricky guy!" He shakes his head as he repeats himself.

I fold my menu and place it on the table with a smile.

"Sometimes a guy is just having lunch, Lou, but today I can tell it's business. Do you want to speak up now so we can enjoy our lunch?" I'm not being rude or anything-- the FBI only takes me out to lunch if they have questions.

"Fine, Pete." He lifts his glass of water for a big swig. "You know the drill well enough by now I guess." The glass gets plunked back down, and he sets his elbows right on the table, interlacing his fingers. He looks serious, but I know this to be his working face. He wasn't mad or anything, just doing his job. "We got more notice of some large sums of money moving into your accounts. You know why?"

Of course I know, it's my money, after all. I smile at him, having anticipated the question, just as I had anticipated the call for lunch after the funds had been transferred. "It's my money, Lou. Some is from a huge commercial sale, which is going into the purchase of a large property overseas."

"Avoiding the capital gains tax, are you?" He wanted to show he was following the conversation.

"Yup, and I'm moving other funds from one account to another to have better access for a couple of pretty substantial stock investments."

He seems to want more of an explanation, even though I really don't have to give him anything else. These transactions are completely legal. I toy with the idea of not telling him anymore, but he is an old friend.

"I am going to be investing a large sum of money into one company in particular. I'm finally going to invest in the technology market. I guess these computers are here to stay, unfortunately." I wave my hand dismissively. Honestly, it's such a small amount of money in the scheme of my actual fortune, but the FBI flags accounts with cash deposits of over ten thousand, and they always have to question the owner about the origin of the funds.

He seems satisfied with the explanation. "Okay, sounds exciting, but a little out of your sphere of expertise." He's referring to my real estate brokerage. Lou knows next to nothing about my holdings and investments.

"I'm willing to take a chance-- why not? Seems like if I sit and wait while they work out some growing pains I will make a decent return. But mostly I like the young girl who wants to learn more about the tech industry, and investment in the stocks." My smile proves my sincerity. "She's beautiful, great body, good head on her shoulders."

"Just the way you like 'em, smart and pretty." Lou glances at the waiter to come over.

"Beautiful," I correct him.

"You wouldn't be talking about that young assistant of yours, would you?" Lou thinks he's so clever.

It's hard enough to make people understand that sex can be only sex, that you don't need to be in love or married or committed to only one person in order to spend intimate time together-- then, to have to try to explain that our sexual relationship was only one facet of a much larger gem? I trust her instinct for people, and therefore I trust her instinct for business. Luckily, I'm saved the need to try to explain any of this when the server shows up.

"Gentlemen, would you like to order?" George is the maî·tre d' here, but when I dine at this club he takes special pride in serving my table.

He's been working here ever since I can remember. His stark white hair stands out against his dark skin; he must be in his seventies by now, but he still gets up every morning and puts on a crisp tuxedo to come here and serve guests in the utmost style. He makes sure to rush over whenever I walk in. I always get a, "Hello, Mr. Pete, right this way!"

Places with this much class are few and far between these days. I make sure this club stays above water with generous donations along with my monthly membership dues. There are old clubs like this all over the world, but this one in my home state is still my favorite.

"I'll have the salmon," says Lou.

"And I'll take the seafood chowder to start. Why don't you follow that with a grilled chicken Caesar salad." As I finish ordering, I motion to George with my pointer finger. He moves closer to me and I extend my hand to shake his. "Thank you, as usual."

The maî·tre d' takes my hand. "Always a pleasure to serve you and your friends, Mr. Pete." The large bill in my hand slides into his, then he moves his hand to his pocket. You see, tipping at the club isn't necessary-- all the fees are covered in our monthly dues-- but I always like to tip anyway. In a place where the service is fast and friendly, I'm always seen and cared for first. A nice perk, and the way I like it, being first place and the best.

Feeling that the opportunity had arisen, at this point in our conversation I decide to tell my old friend my intentions. "It's going to be a while before we can have lunch again."

"Why's that?" He looks a little concerned.

I hold up my hand to assure him. "Nothing's wrong, I'm just thinking of staying down in the Caribbean through the winter."

"Seems..." He pauses. "a little low key for you."

"Not too low key. I've got a couple companies down there. And there's the young, smart, gorgeous element."

Lou gets a goofy grin. "Thinking about settling down again, buddy?"

I snort. "I'll never get married again. Barb was my one and only wife."

Lou looks down at the table cloth. "She was something real special."

I change the subject. "Come on, old friend, what's wrong with living it up now and then? I'm old enough to retire, and so are you. Don't tell me you're not thinking about it." Let's turn the conversation away from my late family.

"I would love to, but I've got one more kid to put through college first." He scratches his head. "My littlest girl Jane-y is in her freshmen year at Yale. Darn smart kid. Fucking expensive school!"

I laugh out loud. "Well I never did get my degree, but I got to teach at the university. Had a good time, too, teaching those investment classes. I got a kick out of those kids trying to call me professor!"

"Never got a degree, and look how good you've got it. Wonder if we're all doing it wrong?"

My soup arrives with a basket of fresh rolls and whipped butter. The extra carbs are a welcome thing today after such an intense morning workout at the boxing gym.

"Nothing wrong about it, just didn't seem to have the time for college. What with the Navy, a wife, a kid running around, and a company to run!"

Lou sighs. "I still remember how smart that boy of yours was! Even when he was a toddler!"

Back to my family again. The man's relentless. Then again, he had known us pretty well back then. Lou even offered to help keep the son of bitch who stole them from me behind bars longer. But I had told him no. God, or karma, or whatever balancing act the universe supports, would take care of that waste of human flesh. I made sure of that. I don't need Lou nosing around. He probably suspects more than he actually knows, but there is no surprise on my part when Lou lowers his voice and narrows his gaze. "I don't know what happened to that criminal after he was let out, but I hope he suffered for what he stole from you." Lou shakes his head again. "It's just not fair, Pete-- you should have had decades more with them."

I stop him there by clearing my throat. "You are right there, my friend. I've never been the same."

Finally, Lou leaves it alone, knowing this is as far as the conversation should go.

I drop the roll in my hand. All of a sudden I have no appetite.

1995
Elaine:

"There isn't much to tell." This is what Pete says when I ask him about the day his son was born.

Then he launches into a Navy story.

"By early January in 1959, we were ready for a three month stay at sea. Barb was pregnant and due to have our baby in late March. So it was possible I would miss the birth.

"I was headed back to the Caribbean on a springboard cruise. We had lovingly nicknamed these trips south, whiskey cruises, because we would take the opportunity to make a little money on the side, sneaking cheap whiskey back to the States on our boats.

"You could bring back a gallon of whiskey legally, but, shit, we would fill that whole storage room. We made a killing selling the stuff back home.

"I remember this one night the Captain went down for ice cream. It was my job to stock and keep track of the storage room, so my ass was on the line. A bunch of us were playing cards when the Cap walked in and declared his intentions for ice-cream. I figured my gig was up, and thought about jumping and swimming home.

"I knew he would notice the whiskey because earlier that day one of the bottles smashed so the storeroom smelled something awful of alcohol. But the Captain, he never said a word to us. He didn't even look at us as he walked out with his ice-cream. He probably didn't want to deal with disciplining the entire crew. But everyone was shitting their pants."

This is the point at which Peter dissolves into laughter over the fond memory.

Then he tells me how after three months at sea, he came home just in time. Barbara was living in the house by the base. He got home at night, and the next morning Barb had the baby. March 28th, 1959.

"Back then," he says, "the woman would go to the hospital, and they'd put her to sleep and she'd have the baby."

I guess Pete brought her to the hospital in the morning and then went off to work on the base, and when he went to the hospital that afternoon it was to meet his already born son: Peter Rich, Jr.

> *"Right after we got married I went to church with Barb and she says to me, 'Why aren't you singing?' So, I start to sing, and she elbows me saying, "Well you don't have to make fun!' I tell you, I wasn't making fun! It's true, I have a horrible singing voice! She informed me I never had to sing again."*

March 1959

Pete:

I hadn't seen her in months, and I knew she would be heavy from carrying our child. I had been trying to prepare myself for what that might mean. Had she lost her swimmer's figure? Would she be bitter because of my long stay at sea? Would she have lost her good mood? That soft smile she always wore, as if she were at every moment making some sort of private joke at the whole world's expense? She was so young. But we had done the right thing: we were married.

I pulled up to the little white house, there was a young oak tree in the yard. I could see she had added curtains to the windows, but otherwise the house looked much the same. It was early March, but the windows were cracked open a little, and I smiled at the thought of Barb needing to let in the ocean air. "The salt air is good for you," she would always tell me. Suddenly I couldn't wait to see her. I turned off the truck.

The sound of waves and movement on the water washed the landscape.

Hoping to surprise her, I went around back, thinking maybe the doors to the porch were open like the windows. And there she was, standing in the yard, with her back to me holding her pregnant belly, staring at the gray sea and swaying to the peaceful music of the waves.

If I had been worried about still finding this woman attractive, I tell you there was no reason for it. She was my same Barb, hair tied up in one of my old bandannas, looking glorious as the early evening moonlight shone down on her.

I must have made some sort of movement toward her, because she turned those baby blue eyes to me.

The short distance between us was gone in seconds.

No one could kiss like her. She was all soft and hard in the right places, sweet to taste and so eager. Eager for everything, to please and be pleased, to make love repeatedly forever and ever. She used to say, "I could do that again, forever and ever!"

I pulled her back to look at her. It's hard to describe how I felt in that moment, but the baby put it perfectly. Our excitement was infectious.

"Junior's excited!" She gasped and took my left hand to place it on the top of her belly, letting me feel the life inside her.

I kissed her again and searched her body with my hands. I kissed her shoulder, her strong and milky white arms. I kissed her long, soft fingers.

I could tell she was happy for the attention after so long apart. Her face glowed and her hair shimmered in the blue twilight. She looked like a mermaid, a siren out of the old sea tales come to entice me.

I found myself proud of her body. I liked it. She looked perfect, healthy and happy and carrying my little junior.

That kind of knowledge, it does something to a man, you know. I had to get her inside or else the neighbors would see more than their fair share of my fair wife. We walked together towards the little seaside house, tangled up together as we would be in bed.

"Junior?" I smiled, thinking about how people always try to guess the sex of the baby before it's born, and how often they are wrong.

"Yeah, Junior. I figure, girl or boy, with your looks, my smarts and all that money, they are going to be just as troublesome as you are." She smiled up at me through her lashes.

"You have no idea how troublesome," I practically growled.

As was always the case, I just couldn't keep my hands off her. We were insatiable. There was no point in all the years of our marriage when that ever changed. Maybe it was the time apart, maybe we were sex crazed--who cares? We were happy, we never had fights, and we knew exactly how to please one another.

We didn't have long to wait for our little Junior. The very next morning Barb woke me and asked me to bring her to the hospital. She was very calm, but I knew it was time. Soon we would bring home our baby.

"People like to be special."

1958-1960
Pete:

For the first couple of years we were married, after our son was born, Barbara and I acquired a multifamily property nearly every month. That's twelve houses per year with two or three apartments in each. When the majority of them were rented out we made a killing, and they were nice enough homes, so it wasn't too difficult to keep them full, especially the units near the university. This was a good time for us. These multifamilies gave us a steady and reliable cash flow, which really made us look good on paper.

I still had my construction company, and had also taken Barb's advice and built a huge commercial complex at a busy intersection in our hometown. Aside from her work at the university, Barb got very efficient at keeping the financial books for all our assets. She kept track of all the rent checks and money coming in, and all the checks going out. She took ten percent of everything we made and set it aside in a savings account for safekeeping. If I sold a new house and made a three-thousand-dollar profit, she would squirrel away three hundred.

She had quite a bit of money saved up after a year. We had both grown up pretty darn poor, so having this safety net gave her a sense of security.

Not that she needed one. We were making money hand over fist. I was still working with Mr. Bob and Mr. Burt. I made the two of them a lot of money. We were a good team.

Even when we first started out and I was still a kid, they always treated me like an equal. Burt trusted me with his money. Then there was Bob who taught me about banking and real estate investing. Those two believed in me a hundred percent because when I said to them I was going to do something I made sure to do it and do it well, with a smile.

In May of 1960, I bought from Mr. Bob a one hundred acre parcel for subdivision, and another one hundred acre parcel for me and Barb.

I wanted to build her a palace, but she wanted a modest house.

"I don't want to flaunt it!" she told me.

"Flaunt what?!" I laughed at her. "How rich we are? How hard you work? You deserve a castle!"

"I just want a normal house, Pete." She put her foot down.

"Okay, dear. Whatever you say." I wouldn't have liked to live in a big fancy house, anyway.

"Oh!" She wanted normal, but not average. "But two bathrooms!"

People say building houses with your spouse can ruin a marriage. Not with us. We agreed on everything, mainly because she trusted that I could build a strong house, and I trusted her with everything else. You know what they say about happy wives!

I remember the day the fireplace was finished. It was a real work of art. In the living room from floor to ceiling stretched this fieldstone fireplace. Barbara had insisted on hiring a local man by the name of Mr. Cal to build it, and he took stones from some of the hundred-year-old stone walls that stretched across our land. The fireplace at least looked as if it could have been from a castle.

Then Mr. Eddie and his brother Nick did all the woodwork. The large country kitchen was full of windows and we built four big bedrooms. It's hard to know if Barb was trying to make up for our frugal time in the seaside house, or if she wanted to fill all the rooms with a big family. Either way she insisted on the four bedrooms.

In turn I insisted every product put into the house be the best quality: all hardwoods, real tile in the bathrooms, and big mullioned windows to let in the sunlight.

I had the master bedroom and bath put on the east side of the home, and the remaining bedrooms were opposite. This would afford us a little more privacy. I chose east thinking of the early morning sunshine that would shine through those big windows. The blue-grey tile I chose mimicked ocean waves on a cloudy day. My dreams were fulfilled the first time I saw Barb bathing in the early morning rays, her stormy blue eyes dancing with the loveliness of it all.

When all was said and done, we ended up with a truly beautiful house, sitting atop a gentle hill, nestled into the trees just a bit. You had to drive over a small bridge built over a wide babbling brook to reach the home. There was a four car garage that housed my vehicles and motorcycle, and an equipment shed, too.

There was a brook like I said, and down a way on the other side of the land was a pond where Barb liked to take Pete Jr. and go fishing. But there wasn't a good place to swim, so I put in a long and narrow lap pool so Barb could keep swimming. It was a saltwater pool, and heated so she could swim late into the season.

Just before Thanksgiving in 1960, we moved away from our little seaside house into that lovely home. I was about to celebrate my twenty-first birthday.

1995

Elaine:

"See that rock wall along the road?" Pete was driving us through town.

"It's amazing." I wasn't kidding. It was a beautifully crafted wall. About shoulder height, very wide and level on top, even though it followed the dips and turns of the hilly countryside.

Pete continued, "The story goes, there was this rich man, a lawyer in town, who was an alcoholic. This was a long time ago before cars. Well, he liked to walk into town and drink himself silly and then walk home. They say he had that wall built so that he could walk to and fro without getting his feet wet."

I laugh, but think that it could be a plausible story. The settled rocks look as though they'd been there forever, but it's still sturdy and hasn't settled or shifted at all.

"We should walk the whole thing someday." I smile at the idea, as does Pete.

He says to me, "I have walked on that wall many times." Of course he has.

He's been kind of quiet all day, lost in his thoughts. I hadn't thought anything of it until we pulled into the cemetery.

In a split-second I knew where we were and why, and the truth of it hit me in the gut. I was simultaneously honored and horrified. It was the cemetery in his hometown. We were here to see Barbara.

We didn't speak at all. He just pulled the Rolls Royce up to a small but sturdy granite monument. He left the car running and the driver's side door open, as if he might need to escape quickly.

We were in a meadow full with gentle green hills, and the sun was shining. All the gorgeous New England mountains rolled around in the distance, but all I could concentrate on was the sudden cold feeling in my chest.

The slab is a chipped granite cross on a large pile of stones. Etched deep into the surface of the grey shrine was the family name:

RICH

On the ground were not one but two flat ground-level tombstones. It was horribly sad to be there in person, to see her name printed out, this woman I had never met but felt I knew so well.

Barbara Rich
1941-1967

Twenty-five. She was twenty-five. I'm the same age now. The harsh finality of that engraved date brought with it layers of sadness. Each of the wonderful stories Pete had shared with me became tinged with a desperate ache for everything left undone.

The second stone gave me a momentary shock. It was Pete's stone, and there was no final date yet, just a blank space:

Peter Rich
1939-

Barbara and Peter Rich would be buried side by side. Here were their two stones, but where... I looked around searching for the other stone that I knew would be somewhere close by.

He was there. Pete was standing silently on the opposite side of the monument, looking down at the short-clipped grass.

I broke the silence with a sad sigh.

How strange it is that he had brought me here. Nobody knows much about Pete-- he's a private man. Even in this town where he grew up, people didn't know him as one of the richest men in the world. Here he was a respected businessman who had started with nothing and built a good life here for his young family.

The small stone at our feet said,

Peter Rich, Jr.
1959-1967

"He would have been thirty-six on Sunday." Peter's sudden words make me jump.

"Oh," was all I could get out. Now I knew why we were here. Not just at the cemetery, but home, in the States. It was the anniversary of their death. This is why he came home once a year, not for the charity function, not even for business. Those were all cover stories. He was here to visit his family.

Peter:

The first night when we brought our baby boy home, Barbara went to bed and I let her sleep. She needed rest and recuperation. All night I held my son. He was a good sleeper, not fussy or anything, but holding him seemed better than putting him down. I never wanted to put him down.

He was so perfect it was hard not to just stare at him. We were still in the little house by the sea then, and I remember swaying back and forth to the ocean's moonlit lullaby. That first night, I stood watch over my little family and planned all the things we would do together. There would be many 'firsts' over the years.

We got to a few 'firsts', but only a few. His first steps. That was a good day. I'll always remember his happy face and outstretched arms as he stumbled his way toward me, saying "dadada".

Then there was the first day of school when he was five years old, and the Christmas when he got his first BB gun. I think he was six that year. He was still a toddler when I watched Barb teach him how to swim. Our first camping trip, little Pete must have been three or four--we did a lot of camping.

I took him hunting the first time when he was seven, and I promised we'd go again for deer season. But it all stopped at eight. I got no more firsts after that.

It had been a good couple of years. Our subdivision on Mr. Bob's one hundred acre parcel had been completed in record time. The money from that development coupled with some amazing investments on Barb's part, helped us to acquire our first high-rise. I didn't see any sense in slowing down, and after the first building in New York, I went on to purchase buildings in Boston and Hartford.

Business was excellent and little Pete was growing like a weed, so it only made sense to Barb that we have another baby. She told me she had been praying for another baby, and shouldn't I go to church with her to pray? I never went to church with them, although they went every Sunday.

In 1967 when my son was eight and Barbara was twenty-five, they got into the car after church and never made it home. A drunk driver crossed the centerline and hit my wife's car head on. Barbara had been four months pregnant. And suddenly they were dead. Quick as anything, it was all over.

My life was forever changed.

It was odd they weren't home from church when I got back to our house. I called out for them, but received no answer.

Barb was teasing me with a fresh baked apple pie. She had left it resting on the counter to cool, with a note nearby that warned me to keep my hands off the wonderful dessert. It said,

Dear Pete: Don't eat the pie.
It's for Sunday Dinner.
(No, not even just one little piece!)

I remember smiling at her conversational note. She knew me so well, and if she wasn't so worked up over how special dinner was that night I probably would have stolen a piece.

We were going to let our families know about the new baby that evening. Barb liked to have our parents over on Sundays, and she knew that her announcement would make this one memorable. She was excited to tell them about our happy news. She hoped it was a baby girl. When I think of the little lost baby, I always think of her as my little girl.

As it turns out, I never ate any of it. It just sat there over the next few days slowly rotting.

The next few days went by like normal days do, but they weren't normal. I was burying my family. The details of those days are vividly imprinted in my memory.

Mr. Del took care of the funeral arrangements at his funeral home. It was a huge Victorian house, with the first floor being the funeral parlor and Mr. Del's family living upstairs. There's a huge oak tree in the middle of the circular drive. The tree's still there today.

Hundreds of people came to the wake. We knew so many people; Barb had touched many lives with her giving, open personality and infectious laughter.

They gave heartfelt condolences and they brought flowers. Barb loved flowers and most people knew it. But their flowers didn't compare to the white roses and hydrangea I had arranged.

The pale blue hydrangea were from our garden, I picked them myself. I nearly killed the bushes, it took them a long while to recover, but that didn't matter. Then I brought all the hydrangea Barb had cultivated over the years to the local flower shop and told them to add white roses. Hundreds of white garden roses, which stand for love and purity.

I've never seen more flowers in one place, all sorts of flowers in every color imaginable. She would have loved to see and smell it.

They had matching caskets, Pete Jr. and Barb. Mr. Del had done a wonderful job on both faces. They looked so peaceful.

The funeral took place the next day at the Episcopal church where we had been married nine years beforehand. It was where Barb sang in the choir, and where little Pete took Sunday school, and where he got to ring the church bell.

The reverend who had married us conducted the service. Every seat in the church was taken. I wondered about our shotgun wedding then. Seeing all the people and all the flowers assembled in one place, it struck me that I never asked Barb if she was disappointed in our small private ceremony. Would she have liked a big white wedding? Why hadn't I ever thought to ask her that? If only I could have talked to her again, if only...

When the procession left for the cemetery, every street was blocked off by the police department. Mr. Del had gotten me a three-grave plot in the new cemetery, one for Barbara and our unborn child, one for little Pete, and one for me.

I am one of those people who never cry, but I sure did cry that day. As they were lowered into the earth, I made a promise right then and there that I would kill the drunken son of a bitch that took them from me. This new resolve centered me. I felt composed again: I had a job to do.

The reception afterwards saw a new Peter Rich. My crying was over. I would never cry again for the rest of my life.

Things were a blur for a while after that. My crews went back to work. I hired a foreman to run things for me while I set things straight. Barb used to help me with the business, now that was not an option.

The plan was simple: first revenge, then go back to work and work like never before. I knew I would never marry again, so my focus would be on building the empire Barb and I had set out to build. I would not let the loss and pain take over. I would fight through it. I still feel the loss every day. Whenever I hear a boy child call out to his father, "Dad!" Junior is there in my minds eye. Or if a man calls his lady 'honey', I think of sweet Barb rolling her eyes at my jokes, but giving in with her easy smile.

It's a terrible thing to lose a child, to remember what it felt like to hold the innocent baby in your arms while they sleep and feel their complete trust in you. The first time you hear them call you, "Dadada". These are things no person should have to lose.

There were so many things we never got to do. I'd never teach my son to drive, or watch him graduate school. Maybe he would have joined the Navy, maybe he would have been a father one day. He could have. He could have been anything.

My dad came to me and said he would take care of the bastard who killed them, but I said no.

I didn't want him to take care of him. There are some things a person must do alone. A secret is only a secret when one person knows.

I was still the only one who knew what had happened to those two divers in the North Atlantic. The captain and crew always suspected, but they never heard a peep from me. Those two divers were dead in minutes. When a person's lungs fill with water it's all over, but there is a moment in time when they know they are about to die. I wanted the son of a bitch to know, I wanted him to feel death grab hold of him. I wanted him to be terrified, and then I wanted him to die. Leaving the funeral that afternoon, my plan was already complete. I knew how to get my revenge.

"There are things you don't know anything about, honey, and it's hard for me to explain. There are things that need to be done regardless of the consequences. I live by my own set of rules, not society's."

1995
Elaine:

My watch reads 6:37 PM. The event is scheduled to start at 7:00. I've been here for a couple hours just to be sure everyone is doing what they should be. I've been planning for the last year, but after visiting the cemetery, there is a tinge of bitter sweetness to this fundraiser.

Today was the twenty-eighth anniversary of the car crash that had killed Pete's growing family and here we were having a big party. I'm not a religious person, but for a moment I pause to think that if Barb were in heaven it would probably be good for her to know we were doing so much to support her shelter. That relaxes me a little.

I'm struck suddenly, as I often am when reflecting on Barb, at how amazing this young woman must have been. In a situation where most people would have done nothing, she had done so much. Many people see hurt and abuse around them and turn a blind eye, but Barb had taken action against it. It probably never even occurred to her that building a home for women and children wasn't a completely normal thing for a person to do. They needed a place to stay, they needed food and comfort, and she made sure they got it. No questions asked.

This organization helped people build new and better lives, like Barb and Pete did for themselves when they were so young. Fighters, that's how I think of them; they never gave up. Now her legacy was living on, the shelter and the scholarship program expanded into a huge organization that helped hundreds every year.

And of course, there's Mr. Amazing himself, my boss and my friend. It's almost crazy to think that by the time Peter was my age he was a multimillionaire who owned banana plantations on exotic islands. It was astounding how much the young couple accomplished together in such a short time. Even so, with all the money, prosperity, and glamour they could have flaunted, instead they made time to stay a part of this community. To protect it and help it heal.

I look around at the venue and realize that in a short time the room would be full of many of the people Barb would have interacted with on a daily basis, her friends and neighbors. Now I am certain that holding this event tonight is a good thing. We were here to honor them.

Tonight is a balancing act of organization, so I need to stay focused. I want very much for everything to go off without a hitch.

I've double checked the schedule of food courses with the catering staff. I want them to serve tonight's meal not all at once but in stages that would allow for dancing and conversation between the courses. But not too slowly, or else we could be here all night.

The sound system was up to snuff, and the music I requested months ago is set to sync relatively well with the pattern of food delivery.

There isn't much left to do except begin greeting guests. Everything seems to be going according to plan, which is how I planned it, of course.

I dash into the bathroom to pull on my nylons. They are always the last part of my outfit to go on, in an attempt to prevent runs for as long as possible. I always get runs. Nylons were invented to go on dolls, it's the only thing that makes sense. How could a real moving, functioning, busy woman be expected to wear the darn things without tearing them to bits? They are practically tissue paper, for goodness sake!

As I bounce around in the public restroom I hear the music start in the distance. I'm sure the guests are starting to arrive by the carload now. We have tables set for over three hundred people tonight.

Peering at myself in the mirror I decide to pull my hair up. It will be much more convenient and out of my way. I check my makeup bag, only six bobby pins. Well, I can manage a quick French twist with those.

In the large rectangular mirror, I apply some sheer pink lipstick and smooth out my hair. Okay. Now it's time to find Pete, if he's even here yet.

Back in the hall, I see him across the room. He's wearing a deep blue suit, perfectly tailored, with a golden silk tie. His cuff links sparkle in the candlelight as he says hello to some old friends.

They look like the children of Mr. Burt, one of the men who mentored Pete as a youth and funded his first house projects. Pete's told me once or twice that Burt's kids got a pretty sizeable inheritance when he passed. I wonder if they knew how instrumental the young Mr. Pete was in forming that huge inheritance. They shook hands enthusiastically enough; they certainly did seem to like him a lot.

Peter makes eye contact with me. We smile. I head to the bar and order a mineral water.

"What, no fun for Elaine tonight?" I turn to the man to my left and laugh.

"Hi, Lou! Nice to see you. Glad you could make it!" I grab his hand and we half shake, half awkwardly hold hands. "How was lunch yesterday?" I retrieve my hand and collect my water. "Keep a gin and tonic ready for me at the end of the night!" I wink at the bartender.

Lou motions to the bartender for another drink. Looks like he's off duty tonight. I check my watch anyway-- we are thirty minutes in and he is on his second drink. Go Lou!

I'll have Pete check on him in a bit so they can swap some war stories. I know from experience Lou likes to reminisce after his third drink. He's harmless, though, a really good guy with an extremely stressful job, so I let him indulge without comment.

He answers my question while swirling the contents of his glass. "Lunch was very nice. Always good to meet up with old friends." Lou's eyes twinkle a little as he looks toward Peter and then back to me. "I hear you are well on your way to becoming quite the business entrepreneur."

"Ah. Well." I wonder, what the heck did they talk about yesterday? "You know Pete's a good mentor. I've been learning a lot." I try to stay focused on the business aspects of our relationship.

"Good. I hope you can do half as well as he has done." Lou's face tightens, and he seems to sober a bit. "But you know, I hope you have better luck in your personal life." He puts his hand on my shoulder in a fatherly way. What *had* he and Pete been talking about? Peter didn't usually talk about his private affairs with anyone, even friends that go as far back as Lou.

There's a commotion by the door. Brewster Newy has just arrived, and he nods toward me as the local press descend on him. Everyone wanted to rub elbows with the big shot CEO Brewster Newy, Harvard professor turned oil tycoon.

Brewster and Pete shake hands. It is so fun for me to watch the local celebrities, politicians, and reporters make such a buzz about Brewster, while Peter fades into the background.

"Brewster Newy, hmph." Lou doesn't look impressed. "Old friends, those two." He waggles a finger back and forth from Pete to Brewster.

"I know," I say. "We've all had lunch a few times." This was a gross understatement; I see Brewster all the time.

"Tricky guy, that one, does a lot of business in Russia and the Middle East. Peter invests in his company, right?"

I try to stay away from talk about Peter's involvement in PB Holdings. "Oh, you know-- he just goes where the oil is, I'm sure." I hesitate, wishing to change the subject but deciding to play dumb instead. "So, is Brewster from around here, then?"

Someone to my right laughs. "From here? What would give you that idea?"

I turn; it's an older woman. Amy? Allison? I can't remember her name, but I know she's a local.

"Alice!" Lou's face lit up. "How are you? Have you met Elaine?"

That's right, Alice. She went to the same high school with Pete and Lou.

"We've met only in passing." Alice shakes my hand. "You are always so busy and on the go." She smiles at me, but I get the feeling she doesn't like me very much.

"Yes, well, my job is very fast paced. Have to keep up with the boss!" I chuckle, trying to break the ice. "It's nice to see you again," I tell her. "I hope you enjoy the party tonight! We've got quite an evening planned!"

"I'm sure you do." Lou pipes up, "Got to if you convinced such a big CEO to come all the way here!"

Back to Newy: "Yup, you know Pete, always with a trick up his sleeve."

Lou laughs aloud. "Tricks, trouble, you name it. He's a funny guy, Pete is."

"Such a shame he never remarried." Alice has a hungry glint in her eye. I notice she is not wearing a wedding ring.

"Oh, Pete's not interested in remarrying. He's too busy seducing younger women." Lou smirks at me, and Alice makes a disgruntled face.

I feel as if I'm about to explode. Not just because Pete's love life was none of their business, but also because this was neither the time nor the place. No way did I want this woman Alice gossiping about Peter, or me for that matter.

Trying to be polite while also saving some shred of my own propriety, I chime in, "Please, of all nights."

I guess our trip to the cemetery was still on my mind. No worries; I'm sure they will think I'm talking about the benefit.

Lou looks at me with narrowed eyes. I suddenly feel as though I'm being interrogated. "You know, I was just thinking about how it was around this time of year. The crash."

Alice gasps. "I'd forgotten! And this shelter was Barb's baby."

Her specific words turn my stomach. The baby. She was pregnant when she died. Peter lost three family members that day.

Lou sees my sorrowful face and he softens, even as Alice continues right on going, "Oh, that horrible drunkard! Whatever happened to him, Lou? Is he still in prison?"

Lou looks at me, searching my face. For what? I wonder at his ability to see through me, to know how much I really do care about and want to protect Peter's privacy. But what is it Lou is looking for now? I don't know anything about the man who killed Pete's family.

"Well, actually, I know for a fact that he only served sixty days in jail and then was released." Lou is still looking at me. "Funny story, he was released and then nobody ever saw him again." He waves his hand in the air and finishes, "He just disappeared."

It feels as though cold water is being poured over my head.

He served only sixty days? After killing two innocent people, and an unborn baby! Why didn't I know this bit of information? What had Peter done when he found out the man who murdered his family was only going to serve two months in jail?

Chunks of the many stories I've been told began to fall into place. What messed up system could release a man like that after sixty days? And Peter, oh god, Peter, the man who made his own rules. I try to control my facial expression as all the pieces fit together. Oh god. Could he have? Yes, I know Pete had killed for our country. But would he have killed for his family. Instantly I know the answer and there is no doubt in my mind. Of course he would, without hesitation.

I ignore Lou and find Peter's eyes staring right at me from across the room. He's been watching us. Watching me. Nothing misses his attention.

He tilts his head to one side, and I feel our silent language working. I see understanding in those eyes, and knowledge. Pete must know that Lou is suspicious. Had he wanted me to figure it out as well? Why? I know he was capable of killing-- that was his job in the Navy, right? He was protecting his crew. But...murder.

Pete's mischievous twinkle falters, and it looks as if he might make a move toward me. It's this, more than anything, that gives me resolve. His one second of weakness. He trusts me. A man made of secrets and I get the biggest one.

I shake my head a fraction, but smile with my eyes so he knows not to worry. Pete's green eyes glow. It's okay. He knows all his secrets are safe with me.

Totally committed that's me. I have the sudden urge to cry or scream, but refrain.

Our eyes stay locked for a few more seconds before he is pulled into conversation with someone else. Lou and Alice have continued their conversation without me. I point to the bathroom and Alice nods at me. Making a B-line for the back door instead, I escape outside into the crisp evening air.

Of course, that's what happened. Now that I think about it, the scenario makes perfect sense. How could I expect anything else from the man who believes in eye-for-an-eye justice, a man who made sure abusive fathers felt the pain they inflicted on their loved ones, a man who spent much of his early adulthood training to be a warrior. I know how much Peter loved his wife and his son, and I know there's no way someone could murder his family and be allowed to live. To Pete this wasn't murder, it was justice.

"The path to hell is paved with good intentions."

1995

Peter:

I'm a little early for the event. My watch says it's nearly 6:40. From the entrance I spy Elaine dashing into the restroom. She's still without stockings and shoes, which means she's just finishing up her work. I watch her disappear barefoot into the lady's room before slipping into the dining hall unnoticed. The room looks very classy, white tablecloths with cream colored roses and candles everywhere.

An old high school acquaintance of mine has arrived early. Her name is Alice. She makes her way over to me.

"Back in town, then?" She kisses each of my cheeks. "Where have your world travels taken you this time?"

"Elaine and I have just returned from Dublin." I see her annoyance at the mention of Elaine, my young and gorgeous assistant. How fun. I decide to tease her more. "Next we will be going to Saint Eustatius to check on my house there and deal with some of my oil investments."

"I don't know why your *assistant*," she said the word assistant a little too bitterly, "has to go with you everywhere." Who does this woman think she is?

"She keeps me organized and manages my whole schedule and my many obligations. How could I travel without her? You aren't jealous, are you Alice?" I tease her and she flashes a killer smile.

"You could take me on one of your trips sometime, Pete. We could pick up where we left off." She touches her pointer finger to one of my shirt buttons and looks up at me through her lashes.

She's been on the prowl for a while, looking for a new husband. We'd slept together years back when she was still married. She told me then she wanted to leave her husband for me. I made it clear I wasn't interested in that. What a mess it would have been! I told her to stay put and not to tell her husband about us. She never said anything, but eventually they did get a divorce.

The first time I'd slept with Alice she'd told me it was better than anything she'd ever had.

She and her unsuspecting husband had just purchased a house from me. The husband was at work while Alice and I had gone to the empty house for a final walkthrough. By the end of our house tour she was perched on one of the kitchen counters with her skirt pushed up over her hips, her panties discarded on the floor. She had on a green blouse which was unbuttoned so that her see through bra was exposed.

Alice said to me that day, "I never thought there really was a G-spot! I've read about it, but..." She shook her head, still breathing heavy.

I teased her then like I tease her now: "I just got lucky, honey."

"No." She shook her head and ran her hands through her hair. "No, that wasn't luck! How did you do that?"

I moved in close, kissing her lips then her biting her nipples through that lace bra. She moaned for me while I made my way up her neck to nibble on her ear and whisper, "Lots of practice."

A tremor of excited pleasure ran through her body as I lifted her up and bent her over the counter. It was time for me to cum. I always make sure the woman orgasms before I do. I don't get laid just to get laid, I do it to make it good, and this was pretty good. She came once more, along with me, and that's when she told me she would leave her husband for me.

No, thank you, not interested!

Back in the present, I flirt with the single lady. Bending to whisper in her ear, "Why would you want to go away with me, Alice? Still having trouble finding that G-spot?"

"You're such a tease," she breathed back at me.

She gets one of my Cheshire Cat grins before I kiss her cheek and say, "I see some old friends. If you'll excuse me..." I don't wait for a response from her, but head over to say hello to Mr. Burt's children.

I always invite them to attend this fundraiser. It's nice to see how they are doing even if it's only once per year.

Elaine reappears. She's put on her black nylons and pulled her hair up to expose her lovely long neck. She's a knockout in her strappy black dress.

As I reconnect with Burt's children, I watch from a distance as my friend Lou approaches Elaine at the bar. She has her polite face on, and as their conversation continues I can tell she's a little flustered. Old codger is probably probing her, but about what? If he was just being nosey about our close relationship that was fine. But if he was searching for other information I might have to intervene. I know Elaine is a keeper of my number one rule, "don't tell tales out of school." But Lou can be a pain in the ass if he wants to be.

A commotion by the door lets me know Brewster has arrived. I walk over to make a show of shaking hands and then I spot Alice joining Elaine and Lou. Every so often one of them glances over at me. I guess I am the topic of conversation.

Elaine had been very quiet all afternoon. Our visit to the cemetery had made her reflective. I could tell she was feeling guilty, but also terribly sad. I understand because the sadness is so common to me. I would give anything to be standing next to my son right now, but I can't.

I can tell from the look on Elaine's face that they are discussing the car crash. Their conversation had turned to this topic that Elaine found so upsetting-- it really was written all over her face. The familiar lines of concern she often wore when she was worrying over the past, listening to a story of mine and putting the pieces together in her head.

It really was only a matter of time. She had all my stories now. She really did know everything.

It was Lou, of course, that did it. He was playing detective, looking for a reaction. He's probably telling them the drunkard had never been seen after he was released from prison; he's looking at Elaine.

I see it happen. Lou's words have a strong effect on Elaine: her whole person adjusts. A subtle shift that no one else would have recognized. Lou didn't have a clue, and turns toward Alice to reminisce.

But Elaine is holding her body completely still, as if in shock. I see her silver-grey eyes are alive and fierce working through the stories and the emotions.

She looks to me and across the distance filled with party people we speak to one another without any words. At first I see her anger and confusion.

I falter for a moment at the implications of someone knowing my secret, really knowing, not just suspicions. This is new territory for me, after remaining silent for so long.

Suddenly Elaine settles and signals to me all is well. She adjusts her posture slightly with a movement of her head and a slight relaxing of her eyes.

I turn back to my guests. My secret is safe. She is committed to the company. She is committed to me.

Our eyes stay locked for a few more seconds. There is no more conversation, just a peaceful feeling of contentment and understanding. Brewster makes a comment about the current real estate market and our conversation continues.

    The man who killed my family was a goner the second I found out. I could have killed him before the trial, but I waited and planned. If the bastard disappeared before his trial, there would have been an investigation. The authorities would have searched for him. So, I waited. I didn't have to wait too long, however, since the legal system at the time was very lax about drinking and driving.

    The son of a bitch went to trial and pleaded guilty. He got sixty days in jail and lost his license for one year. He had injured people before, but never killed. This was his third offense. I would make sure it was his last.

"Revenge is a dish best served cold."

1967
Pete:

Patience, they say, is a virtue. Throughout the trial, I watched quietly. During the sixty-day prison sentence, I waited, contemplating.

When the son of a bitch did get out of jail he headed straight for a bar. Still I waited for the right moment. He was in that bar a couple of hours, drinking himself silly. That's how I got him. That bastard staggered out of the dive bar fumbling with the keys to his truck. He didn't give a shit about the law, or the dead he left behind him. He was drunk and without a license, and here he was, not even a day out of prison about to hit the road again.

I didn't really care at this point if anyone saw us, but I double checked anyway, making sure no one was around. I clocked him a good one and down he went, a crumpled mess on the ground. He went into the back of my van that I used for fishing and hauling equipment. I had a canvas tarp laid out. There I gagged and hogtied him before climbing into the driver's seat.

Back at my house, I pulled right into the garage and closed the door. He had wet and shit himself. He struggled with the restraints and tried to yell, but it was muffled from the gag.

If you want to go fishing for sharks, you bait them with chum. I had moved a large chum barrel into my garage for the purpose of hiding this bastard.

Saying nothing by way of explanation I dumped him into a chum barrel. The smell of the fish bait at the bottom of the barrel masked the smell of his bodily waste and fear.

I wanted him alive, so I made sure he could breathe before I climbed back into the driver's seat and headed to the shore.

I had kept Barb's boat docked at a fairly private dock right next to a charter boat captain's ship. People were used to seeing me late at night and before light very early in the morning. No one would give a second thought about me hauling a big cooler or a barrel of chum onto my fishing boat.

It was three in the morning when I loaded the barrel onto the "RICHCO" and fired up the twin diesels.

A couple of crew from one of the fishing charters, saw me and waved as I set off. The muffled sounds from the chum barrel couldn't even be heard over the roar of the engines.

Two hours later saw me out past the two hundred fathom curve. It was just starting to get light. The sun hadn't appeared yet; it was just the time of morning when the sky lightens to pale pinks and wispy blues. There wasn't another boat in sight.

I dumped the chum barrel out right onto the deck. He was nice and ripe. The fish would be on him quickly. I wrapped a thick chain and secured it around his ankles so he would sink to the bottom. He was shaking all over in fear. I wanted him to be afraid, but also to know why he was about to die. He struggled as I lifted him by the shirt and looked into his eyes.

During the trial, I had made sure to be present every day. This man knew my face well. I said nothing at all, but recognition flashed in his eyes. He looked around at all the water and began to struggle and moan again.

He gave up kicking after I dragged him to the transom and opened the tuna door. He just looked up at me, wide eyed and fearful. Breaking my silence at last, I spoke to the man that murdered my unborn baby, my eight-year-old son, and my best friend, sweet beautiful Barb. "You will die now for your crime."

Though his one miserable life hardly made up for what had been lost, justice should prevail. This man had lost his driver's license and gone to jail for a few weeks. That is not justice. After hearing my words, I could see the fight leave him-- what was left of it after so many years attached to a bottle.

I kicked his body into the ocean and watched it quickly disappear beneath me. Once again, the dark water ate up the body sinking away from my sight. In seconds he was gone. I've watched my enemies float away so many times before.

Drowning is quicker than most people think, especially if you're scared or unprepared. After the first breath on the way down, he would be dead. I guessed he'd have about thirty seconds of life left to him, just enough time to realize he was a goner.

In a week's time, the fish would reduce him to a skeleton.

On my way in, I did not stop to fish, but did throw in the green crabs for the black fish.

1995
Pete:

Memories. Memories can keep you together, or they can tear you apart. My memories do both. The strength I receive from my lost family is incredible. My daily work is made possible by them. It still pains me to be without them, but every day I become more grateful for the time we did have together, and the beautiful stories I collected and hold safe within me.

I'm standing in the sand on Statia as the sun is beginning to drop below the horizon. My boat is in the water just off to the left. We've arrived only an hour ago. Elaine is in the house on a call with Karen. Cell phones! People don't know how to relax and enjoy the moment lately.

On my honeymoon, there had been no phones in the beach houses. Now Elaine had one in her hand at all times. She could always be reached, even on this remote and tiny island. Thirteen square miles.

Behind me is the Quill national forest, my old banana plantation. The dormant volcano is still home to the lush rainforest my boy used to play in. Little Pete.

Giving the land away had been an easy decision because this had been Barb's favorite place, the sandy beach where she felt free under the sun. I wanted a piece of this place to remain as she had remembered it, untouched by human development, secluded. An easy place to be alone and find peace.

The sunlight on water always reminds me of her and I remember as if it were yesterday: Barb's big smile as she dropped her panties and bounced off onto the powdery white sand. She laughed the whole time, in nervous ecstasy.

The fantasy sweeps me away while the warm salty breeze pulls me toward the sea. I would have followed that woman anywhere that day. As a matter of fact, I did! I still remember my shock as the warm water hit me. I was still wearing my clothes! But it didn't matter. I was so eager to reach her, touch her, make love to her.

There. That's a good memory, me half-dressed with the waves hitting me as my new bride clung to me, showing me without busy words just how much she loved me.

"Welcome home." It was a woman's voice, a low sensual voice. I blink a few times, clearing my head, and turn to Elaine. She's changed into a swimsuit and has a shawl tied around her waist. I smile at her, thinking how nice it is that she knows so much about me and my journey.

If she merely keeps the stories close and uses them to fuel her own passionate journey through life, then so be it. At least I have passed on something to someone.

I'm not in the mood to talk, so I nod and squeeze her hand, and we take a stroll down the beach together in silence while my past dances around in my head. My grandfather, and the rest of my family, all the conquests both for sex and business... Memories of a boy and his mother, and a childhood from long ago...

Elaine's Final Note:

Maybe he always knew I would start writing it down, that deep down I would see this story had to be told. Parts of it have still never been spoken aloud. I've replicated as much as I could from the real and run wild with the bull. Now it's my story, too. As I type these final words I feel relief wash over me and the responsibility of being the carrier of these life events lifts. There should be a record, a witness. A memory. Even if it's only a partial reckoning.

For so long, he used his anonymity to stay safe, a man making dangerous decisions for his country and for his sense of justice. Only a few people in the world have ever known Pete, who he really is and what he has accomplished. Until now.

Peter Rich:

Lives in Tolland County Connecticut. He resides in a lovely house near a small brook that he built decades ago for his family. Now a retired Commercial Real Estate Broker he remains here at this home surrounded by the memories of his wife and son.

Rebekah Salamack:

Met Peter Rich while attending the University of Connecticut. After graduating with a degree in English Literature, she agreed to ghost write Peter's life story, with a few fun additions.

"I thank dear Pete for this opportunity. It has been quite a ride, learning all about his life, and making a dear friend along the way. Also, I would like to dedicate this first book endeavor to my loving husband who without complaint supported me during the long book writing process."

CPSIA information can be obtained
at www.ICGtesting.com
Printed in the USA
BVOW11s0943130517
484069BV00001B/130/P

9 780998 946009